gets you through

KS3

MATHS

WORKBOOK

GILLIAN RICH

About this book

This workbook contains:

- topic-based questions for focused skills practice and to test your understanding of all the concepts on the Key Stage 3 course
- mixed test-style questions to ensure you are well prepared for end of key stage tests and assessments.

Key features

A Quick-fire, multiple-choice questions to get you warmed up.

C Longer, structured questions to test your problem-solving skills and familiarise you with test-style questions. Icons show which of these can be answered with a calculator.

Two pages of practice for each topic.

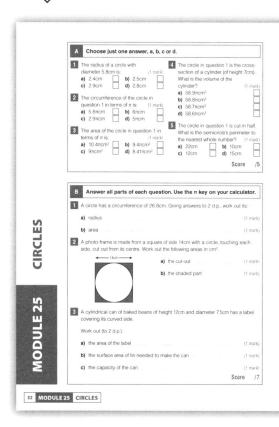

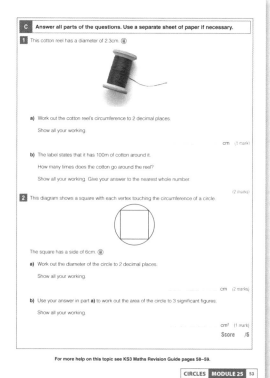

B More challenging short answer questions.

If you need more help, turn to the matching module in the Letts KS3 Success Maths Revision Guide (ISBN 9780008299118).

Mark your answers using the pull-out booklet and record your total scores.

Contents

Number

Algebra

Ratio, proportion and rates of change

Geometry and measures

Probability

Statistics

ACKNOWLEDGEMENTS

The author and publisher are grateful to the copyright holders for permission to use quoted materials and images.

Images are ©Shutterstock.com

Every effort has been made to trace copyright holders and obtain their permission for the use of copyright material. The author and publisher will gladly receive information enabling them to rectify any error or omission in subsequent editions. All facts are correct at time of going to press.

Published by Letts Educational
An imprint of HarperCollinsPublishers
1 London Bridge Street
London SE1 9GF

ISBN: 9780008299125

Content first published 2014
This edition published 2018

10 9 8 7 6 5 4 3

© HarperCollinsPublishers Limited 2018

All rights reserved. No part of this publication may be reproduced, stored in a retrieval system, or transmitted, in any form or by any means, electronic, mechanical, photocopying, recording or otherwise, without the prior permission of Letts Educational.

British Library Cataloguing in Publication Data.

A CIP record of this book is available from the British Library.
Commissioning Editor: Rebecca Skinner

Author: Gillian Rich
Project Management: Fern Labram, Shelley Teasdale and Richard Toms
Editorial: Linda Mellor
Cover Design: Sarah Duxbury
Inside Concept Design: Paul Oates and Ian Wrigley
Production: Lyndsey Rogers
Text Design and Layout: Aptara®, Inc.
Printed in Great Britain by Bell and Bain Ltd, Glasgow

MIX
Paper from responsible source
FSC™ C007454
www.fsc.org

This book is produced from independently certified FSC™ paper to ensure responsible forest management.

For more information visit:
www.harpercollins.co.uk/green

PLACE VALUE AND ORDERING

A Choose just one answer, a, b, c or d.

1 Which is the smallest number in this list? *(1 mark)*

2, –2, –1, 0, 3, 1

a) 2 ☐ b) –2 ☐
c) 1 ☐ d) 0 ☐

2 What number is 5 less than 3? *(1 mark)*

a) 1 ☐ b) –1 ☐
c) 2 ☐ d) –2 ☐

3 Which of the following numbers is one thousand, two hundred and four point nine? *(1 mark)*

a) 124.9 ☐ b) 1024.9 ☐
c) 1204.9 ☐ d) 1042.9 ☐

4 Which symbol is missing between these two numbers? *(1 mark)*

–6   –2

a) ≠ ☐ b) ≤ ☐
c) > ☐ d) ≥ ☐

5 What is the value of the underlined digit?

105$\underline{6}$.32 *(1 mark)*

a) 6000 ☐
b) 600 ☐
c) $\frac{6}{10}$ ☐
d) 6 ☐

Score /5

B Answer each question.

1 What is the value of the underlined digits?

201$\underline{7}$ $\underline{1}$79 $\underline{9}$9.9   3.2$\underline{4}$1

(1 mark)

2 Write these decimals in order, starting with the smallest.

32.4   32.04   32.3   32.024

(1 mark)

3 Write these measurements in descending order.

2162cm   20.25m   2020cm   21 170mm   21.65m

(1 mark)

4 Write < or > between the following numbers.

3.65 ☐ 3.43   41.6 ☐ 46.1   87.204 ☐ 87.02   0.41 ☐ 0.43

(1 mark)

5 Write = or ≠ between the following measurements.

0.42km ☐ 4300m   87.204m ☐ 8720.4cm

363g ☐ 0.363kg   £44.60 ☐ 4406p *(1 mark)*

Score /5

C | **Answer all parts of the questions. Use a separate sheet of paper if necessary.**

1 There are three different ways of making 40p with 10p and 20p coins.

Total 40p

10p coins	20p coins
0	2
2	1
4	0

Complete the table below to show all five ways of making 90p with 10p and 20p coins.

Total 90p

10p coins	20p coins

(2 marks)

2 This is a list of numbers:

  11   12   28   38   46   54   72

a) Write down two numbers from the list which add up to 100. (1 mark)

b) Write down two numbers from the list which have a difference of 26. (1 mark)

c) What is the largest number that can be made by multiplying together two of the numbers on the list? (1 mark)

3 Write the missing numbers in the boxes.

$\boxed{}$ + 0.04 = 1

0.4 + 0.04 = 1 − $\boxed{}$ (2 marks)

4 A four-digit PIN number starts with 7 and ends with 5.

7	?	?	5

The first two digits add up to the same as the last two digits.

Write down all the numbers that this PIN could be. (2 marks)

Score   /9

For more help on this topic see KS3 Maths Revision Guide pages 4–5.

FACTORS, MULTIPLES AND PRIMES

MODULE 2

A   Choose just one answer, a, b, c or d.

1 Which number has a factor of 16? *(1 mark)*
a) 258 ☐   **b)** 112 ☐
c) 596 ☐   **d)** 452 ☐

2 Which number has 215 as one of its multiples? *(1 mark)*
a) 40 ☐   **b)** 15 ☐
c) 43 ☐   **d)** 25 ☐

3 The Lowest Common Multiple (LCM) of 24 and 60 is: *(1 mark)*
a) 90 ☐   **b)** 120 ☐
c) 30 ☐   **d)** 10 ☐

4 The Highest Common Factor (HCF) of 48 and 64 is: *(1 mark)*
a) 14 ☐   **b)** 8 ☐
c) 4 ☐   **d)** 16 ☐

5 Which number has a prime factor of 13? *(1 mark)*
a) 78 ☐   **b)** 87 ☐
c) 93 ☐   **d)** 43 ☐

Score   /5

B   Answer all parts of each question.

1 Look at this list of numbers.

4   5   7   8   14   25   40

a) Write down the multiples of 5. *(1 mark)*

b) Write down the factors of 28. *(1 mark)*

2 Find the prime factors of:

a) 36 *(1 mark)*

b) 48 *(1 mark)*

c) 42 *(1 mark)*

d) 80 *(1 mark)*

3 **a)** What is the Lowest Common Multiple (LCM) of: *(2 marks)*

i) 30 and 45?   **ii)** 12 and 20?

b) What is the Highest Common Factor (HCF) of: *(2 marks)*

i) 40 and 56?   **ii)** 32 and 80?

4 **a)** What is the Lowest Common Multiple (LCM) of 3, 6, 10?

(1 mark)

b) What is the Highest Common Factor (HCF) of 54, 72, 90?

(1 mark)

Score   /12

C **Answer all parts of the questions. Use a separate sheet of paper if necessary.**

1 For each number in the table, write a multiple of that number. Each multiple must be between 100 and 125. The first one is done for you.

a)

Number	Multiple
21	105
30	
28	

(1 mark)

b) Is 8 a factor of 160?

Tick (✓) Yes or No

☐ Yes   ☐ No

Explain your answer.

(1 mark)

2 A is the sequence: 3, 9, 12, 15, 21, 27, ...

B is the sequence: 5, 10, 15, 20, 25, 30, ...

C is the sequence: 1, 2, 3, 4, 5, 6, ...

a) List any primes in sequence A. Explain your answer.

(1 mark)

b) List any primes in sequence B. Explain your answer.

(1 mark)

c) List any even primes in sequence C. Explain your answer.

(1 mark)

3 The numbers 27 and 18 have common factors.

a) List the common factors of 27 and 18.

(1 mark)

b) What is the Highest Common Factor of 27 and 18?

(1 mark)

c) What is the Lowest Common Multiple of 27 and 18?

(1 mark)

Score   /8

For more help on this topic see KS3 Maths Revision Guide pages 6–7.

A — Choose just one answer, a, b, c or d.

1 What is the answer to
116.3 + 27.8? (1 mark)

a) 114.4 ☐ **b)** 101.4 ☐
c) 144.1 ☐ **d)** 41 ☐

2 What is the answer to
457 − 369? (1 mark)

a) 88 ☐ **b)** 86 ☐
c) 112 ☐ **d)** 68 ☐

3 The temperature in Rome at 9°C is
12°C warmer than London. What is
the temperature in London? (1 mark)

a) 0°C ☐ **b)** −1°C ☐
c) −2°C ☐ **d)** −3°C ☐

4 What is $\frac{239}{4}$ as a mixed
number? (1 mark)

a) 59 ☐ **b)** $59\frac{3}{4}$ ☐
c) $45\frac{1}{4}$ ☐ **d)** $54\frac{1}{9}$ ☐

5 What is the answer to $3\frac{3}{4} \times \frac{1}{2}$? (1 mark)

a) $1\frac{5}{8}$ ☐ **b)** $1\frac{1}{6}$ ☐
c) $1\frac{7}{8}$ ☐ **d)** $\frac{3}{8}$ ☐

Score /5

B — Answer all parts of each question.

1 Work out the answers to the following:

a) 406 + 1109 .... (1 mark)

b) 492.6 − 87.8 .... (1 mark)

2 Work out the answers to the following:

a) 43 × 27 .... (1 mark)

b) 576 ÷ 18 .... (1 mark)

3 The temperature is 5°C. Work out the temperature after:

a) a drop of 10°C .... (1 mark)

b) a drop of 10°C then a rise of 17°C .... (1 mark)

4 a) A shopping bag holds $\frac{1}{2}$ kg of apples and $\frac{3}{5}$ kg of carrots is added.
What is the total weight of the bag? .... (1 mark)

b) If $\frac{1}{4}$ kg of carrots is removed, how much does the bag weigh now?

.... (1 mark)

5 Work out the answers to the following:

a) $\frac{1}{3} \times 4\frac{1}{5}$ .... (1 mark)

b) $5\frac{2}{9} \div \frac{3}{5}$ .... (1 mark)

Score /10

1 Write in the missing numbers. The first pair is done for you.

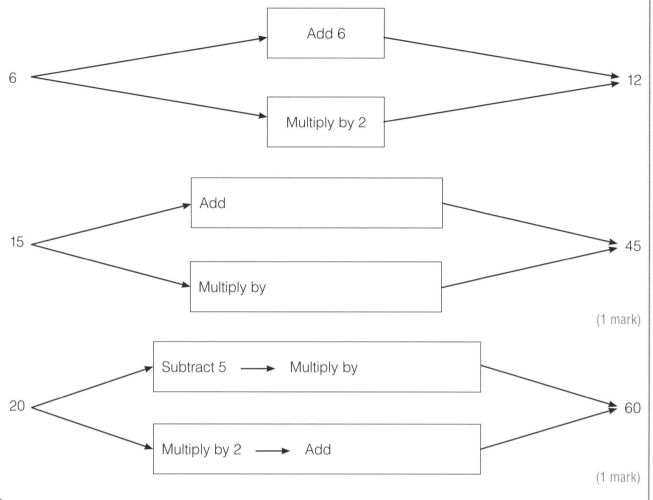

6 → Add 6 → 12

6 → Multiply by 2 → 12

15 → Add → 45

15 → Multiply by → 45

(1 mark)

20 → Subtract 5 → Multiply by → 60

20 → Multiply by 2 → Add → 60

(1 mark)

2 The time difference between London and New York is –5 hours. The time difference between New York and San Francisco is –3 hours.

a) If it is 11:32 in London, what is the time in San Francisco?

(1 mark)

The time difference between London and Beijing is +8 hours. It is 09:15 on Tuesday in Beijing. What is the time and day in:

b) London?

(1 mark)

c) New York?

(1 mark)

d) San Francisco?

(1 mark)

Score   /6

For more help on this topic see KS3 Maths Revision Guide pages 8–9.

A Choose just one answer, a, b, c or d.

1 What is the value of 4^5? (1 mark)
a) 120
b) 20
c) 1024
d) 1025

2 Which is the correct value for $\sqrt{576}$? (1 mark)
a) 22
b) 24
c) 28
d) 26

3 Which of the following equals 86 200 000? (1 mark)
a) 862×10^5
b) 8.62×10^5
c) 86.2×10^{-6}
d) 8.62×10^7

4 Which is $a^2 \times a^3 \times b^2 \times b^6 \times b^{-1} \times c^{-1}$? (1 mark)
a) $a^5 b^7 c^{-1}$
b) $a^{-6} b^{-12} c^{-1}$
c) $a^{-2} b^{-9} c^{-1}$
d) $(abc)^{11}$

5 Which of the following equals $5c^{-\frac{1}{3}}$? (1 mark)
a) $\dfrac{5}{c^3}$
b) $5\sqrt[3]{c}$
c) $\dfrac{5}{\sqrt[3]{c}}$
d) $\dfrac{5}{\sqrt{c}}$

Score   /5

B Answer all parts of each question.

1 Write the value of the following. (2 marks)
a) 6^5 ....
b) 7^0 ....

2 Write the following in full. (2 marks)
a) 3^4 ....
b) $(5^2)^3$ ....

3 Put these numbers into standard form.
a) 0.000 0235 .... (1 mark)
b) 176 300 000 .... (1 mark)

4 Simplify the following.
a) $3 \times p \times p^2 \times pq \times 2q \times qp$ .... (1 mark)
b) $a^2 b^3 c \div ab^2 c^3$ .... (1 mark)
c) $(4x^3)^2 \times (2x^2)^3$ .... (1 mark)
d) $(8e^4)^2 \div 2e^{-2}$ .... (1 mark)

Score   /10

Answer all parts of the questions. Use a separate sheet of paper if necessary.

1 There are two consecutive integers. They are each squared. The squares are added together.

Is the sum odd or even?

Tick (✓) Odd or Even

☐ Odd   ☐ Even

Show proof for your answer.

(1 mark)

2 This table shows data about overseas visitors to the UK for a holiday over a $2\frac{1}{2}$ year period.

Time period	Number of visitors
Jan–Jun 2011	1.4421×10^4
Jul–Dec 2011	1.6377×10^4
Jan–Jun 2012	1.4731×10^4
Jul–Dec 2012	1.6379×10^4
Jan–Jun 2013	1.5239×10^4

a) Which six-month period had the lowest number of visitors?

(1 mark)

b) What was the difference in visitor numbers between 2011 and 2012?

Show all working and give your answer in standard form.

(2 marks)

c) Is there likely to be an increase or a decrease in visitor numbers for the second half of 2013?

Tick (✓) Increase or Decrease

☐ Increase   ☐ Decrease

Explain your answer.

(1 mark)

3 Fill in the missing values in this table.

x	$3x$	$2x^2$
4	12	
3		
		50

(2 marks)

Score   /7

For more help on this topic see KS3 Maths Revision Guide pages 10–11.

A Choose just one answer, a, b, c or d.

1 What is 73% as a fraction? (1 mark)

a) $\frac{73}{10}$ ☐ b) $7\frac{3}{10}$ ☐

c) $\frac{73}{100}$ ☐ d) $\frac{73}{1000}$ ☐

2 What is 0.375 as a percentage?
(1 mark)

a) 3.75% ☐ b) 37.5% ☐
c) 30.75% ☐ d) 0.375% ☐

3 What is $\frac{2}{7}$ as a decimal to 2 d.p.?
(1 mark)

a) 0.27 ☐ b) 0.29 ☐
c) 0.227 ☐ d) 0.277 ☐

4 What is 0.82 as a fraction in its lowest terms? (1 mark)

a) $\frac{41}{50}$ ☐ b) $\frac{42}{50}$ ☐

c) $\frac{82}{50}$ ☐ d) $\frac{41}{100}$ ☐

5 What is £12.60 as a percentage of £20? (1 mark)

a) 6.3% ☐
b) 1.63% ☐
c) 12.60% ☐
d) 63% ☐

Score /5

B Answer all parts of each question.

1 Change these fractions to decimals.

a) $\frac{5}{8}$ .... (1 mark)

b) $1\frac{4}{5}$ .... (1 mark)

2 Change these fractions to percentages.

a) $\frac{9}{16}$ .... (1 mark)

b) $\frac{15}{32}$ .... (1 mark)

3 Change these decimals to fractions.

a) 0.432 .... (1 mark)

b) 0.14 .... (1 mark)

4 Express the first quantity as a percentage of the second quantity.

a) 24mm; 4cm .... (1 mark)

b) 45mins; $2\frac{1}{2}$ hrs .... (1 mark)

c) 425g; 3kg .... (1 mark)

d) 54ml; 1 litre .... (1 mark)

Score /10

C **Answer all parts of the questions. Use a separate sheet of paper if necessary.**

1 This is a square divided into four strips. Each strip has parts of equal width.

a) Use the diagram to work out the missing numbers. The first one is done for you.

If **A** = 100%, **B** = 50%

If **C** = 100%, **B** = ...%

If **D** = 100%, **A** = ...%

If **D** = 100%, **C** = ...%

A		A	
B	B	B	B
C	C	C	C	C
D	D	D	D	D	D

(2 marks)

b) What fraction is **D** of **B**?

(1 mark)

c) What fraction is **A** of **C**?

(1 mark)

2 A group of people were asked if they were considering giving up eating meat.

27% of the group said they were considering giving up eating meat.

21% of these said they might become vegetarian.

What percentage of the original group might become vegetarian? 🔲

(1 mark)

3 Use arrows to show the results to **a)** and **b)** on this number line.

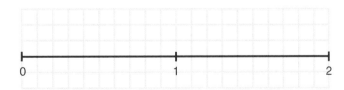

a) $\frac{3}{8} + 1\frac{1}{2}$

b) 3.46 – 2.77

(2 marks)

Score   /7

For more help on this topic see KS3 Maths Revision Guide pages 12–13.

A Choose just one answer, a, b, c or d.

1 Which of the following equals 140 to nearest 10? (1 mark)
a) 134 ☐
b) 145 ☐
c) 136 ☐
d) 146 ☐

2 Which of the following equals 700 to nearest 100? (1 mark)
a) 647 ☐
b) 649 ☐
c) 750 ☐
d) 748 ☐

3 Which of the following equals 2000 to nearest 1000? (1 mark)
a) 1555 ☐
b) 1459 ☐
c) 2500 ☐
d) 1450 ☐

4 What is 3.056 24 to 3 d.p.? (1 mark)
a) 3.056 ☐
b) 3.05 ☐
c) 3.0562 ☐
d) 3.057 ☐

5 What is 4218 to 3 s.f.? (1 mark)
a) 422 ☐
b) 4210 ☐
c) 4200 ☐
d) 4220 ☐

Score /5

B Answer all parts of each question.

1 Round the following to the nearest 100. (2 marks)

a) 365 .... b) 1043 ....

2 Correct the following to 2 s.f. (2 marks)

a) 0.002 154 .... b) 10 650 ....

3 Correct the following to 3 d.p. (2 marks)

a) 2.3218 .... b) 0.067 23 ....

4 Work out the estimated and exact answers (to 2 d.p.) to the following.

a) 1462 ÷ 53 .... (2 marks)

b) 0.83 × 0.902 .... (2 marks)

c) 157 ÷ 8.9 .... (2 marks)

d) 11.2 × 1.2 .... (2 marks)

Score /14

Answer all parts of the questions. Use a separate sheet of paper if necessary.

1 An online encyclopaedia gives this information about the five highest mountains in England.

Mountain	Height (m)
Scafell Pike	978
Scafell	964
Helvellyn	950
Ill Crag	935
Broad Crag	934

a) Which mountain is 930m high to the nearest 10m?

(1 mark)

b) How many mountains are 1000m to the nearest 100m?

(1 mark)

c) The highest mountain in Western Europe is Mont Blanc. Its height is 4807m.

Write the missing value in the following sentence.

The height of Mont Blanc is 5000m to the nearest .... m.

(1 mark)

2 This is the floor plan of a small theatre:

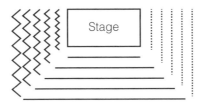

The area with the dotted lines has 40 seats.

a) What is the approximate total number of seats in the theatre?

(1 mark)

b) These are the costs of seats for a Saturday Matinee.

Adult: £18   Adult aged over 60: £15   Child: £10   Student: £12

The theatre is sold out for a pantomime. The audience is made up of $\frac{1}{2}$ adults, $\frac{1}{8}$ students, $\frac{1}{4}$ children and the rest of the people are aged over 60.

Work out how much was taken in ticket sales to the nearest £100.

(2 marks)

Score   /6

For more help on this topic see KS3 Maths Revision Guide pages 14–15.

A — Choose just one answer, a, b, c or d.

1 Which is the answer to
3.257 + 40.38 − 9.045? *(1 mark)*
a) 34.5 ☐ b) 43.637 ☐
c) 52.682 ☐ d) 34.592 ☐

2 Which is the answer to 3 d.p. of
$\dfrac{0.673 \times 4.2}{1.59}$? *(1 mark)*
a) 1.778 ☐ b) 1.7777 ☐
c) 1.777 ☐ d) 1.78 ☐

3 Which is the answer to 4 s.f. of
$\sqrt{5^3 + 3^5}$? *(1 mark)*
a) 19.1833 ☐ b) 19.18 ☐
c) 19.18$\dot{3}$ ☐ d) 19.183 ☐

4 Which is the answer (lowest terms) to
$1\frac{2}{7} \times \frac{4}{9} \times 2\frac{1}{2}$? *(1 mark)*

a) $\frac{4}{7}$ ☐ b) $1\frac{3}{7}$ ☐

c) $1\frac{4}{7}$ ☐ d) $2\frac{3}{7}$ ☐

5 Which is the answer, in standard form,
to $\dfrac{3.52 \times 10^5}{5.3 \times 10^{-2}}$? *(1 mark)*
a) 6.6415×10^7 ☐
b) 6.6415×10^3 ☐
c) 6.6415×10^6 ☐
d) 6.6415×10^{-6} ☐

Score   /5

B — Answer all parts of each question.

1 Calculate the following, giving answers to 3 d.p. *(2 marks)*

a) 6.472×2.04 .... b) $(4.12 + 3.25)(5.02 − 4.33)$ ....

2 Calculate the following, giving answers to 3 s.f. *(2 marks)*

a) £23.78 ÷ 7 .... b) 43.6kg ÷ 2.2 ....

3 Calculate the following, giving answers in lowest terms.

a) $\left(\frac{5}{14} \times \frac{4}{7} \right) \div 3$ .... *(1 mark)*

b) $3\frac{3}{8} − 2\frac{11}{12} + 1\frac{5}{6}$ .... *(1 mark)*

4 Calculate the following, giving answers in standard form.

a) 0.07652×0.34 .... *(1 mark)*

b) $1\,300\,500 \div 3.5$ .... *(1 mark)*

5 Calculate the following.

a) $\dfrac{\sqrt[3]{14.706125}}{5}$ .... *(1 mark)*

b) $\dfrac{6^3 \times 3^3}{5^2 \times 2^5}$ .... *(1 mark)*

Score   /10

Answer all parts of the questions. Use a separate sheet of paper if necessary.

1 The population of Paris is 2 235 963. The population of London is 8 308 369. 🖩

    a) What is the difference in population of the two cities?

                                          (1 mark)

    b) Write the difference in standard form.

                                          (1 mark)

2 Using a calculator, work out the following calculations.

Write down all the digits on the display. 🖩

    a) 2.7^3

                                          (1 mark)

    b) $7^6(2^{-4} \times 4^3)$

                                          (1 mark)

    c) 5.3^5

                                          (1 mark)

    d) $\dfrac{\sqrt{11^2 - 0.5^3}}{4}$

                                          (1 mark)

3 The numbers 1 to 6 are each written on a card. | 1 | 2 | 3 | 4 | 5 | 6 |

They are arranged in different combinations to make the following calculations.

Fill in the missing digits. The first is done for you. 🖩

    a) | 4 | 5 | 6 | – | 1 | 2 | 3 | = 333

    b) | | | | + | | | | = 381

                                          (1 mark)

    c) | | | | × | | | | = 85 796

                                          (1 mark)

    d) | | | | | ÷ | | | = 544.5

                                          (1 mark)

Score   **/9**

For more help on this topic see KS3 Maths Revision Guide pages 16–17.

A Choose just one answer, a, b, c or d.

1 Which of these equals $8ab^2c$? (1 mark)
- **a)** $8 \times a \times b \times c$ ☐
- **b)** $4a \times b \times 2c$ ☐
- **c)** $2ab \times 4ac$ ☐
- **d)** $2a \times 2b \times 2c \times b$ ☑

2 Which of these is $(p^2q)^4$ simplified? (1 mark)
- **a)** p^8q^4 ☑
- **b)** p^6q^4 ☐
- **c)** $p^{\frac{1}{2}}q$ ☐
- **d)** p^2q^4 ☐

3 Which of these is not an equation? (1 mark)
- **a)** $v = u + at$ ☐
- **b)** $y = 3x + 2$ ☐
- **c)** $2a + 3b + 4c$ ☑
- **d)** $2a + b = 2b + a$ ☐

4 Which of the following equals $3(x + 2y)$? (1 mark)
- **a)** $3x + 2y$ ☐
- **b)** $3x + 6y$ ☑
- **c)** $x^3 + 2y^3$ ☐
- **d)** $6xy$ ☐

5 Which of the following is a quadratic expression? (1 mark)
- **a)** $a + 3ab$ ☐
- **b)** $4a + 4$ ☐
- **c)** $a + 2ab + 1$ ☐
- **d)** $a^2 + 2ab + 1$ ☐

Score /5

B Answer all parts of each question.

1 Simplify each of the following into one term.
- **a)** $x \times x \times x \times x \times y \times y \times z$ $x^3 \times y^2 \times z$ (1 mark)
- **b)** $4 \times 3a \times \dfrac{a}{2} \times a$ $12a^2 \times \frac{a}{2}$ (1 mark)

2 Simplify each of the following into one term.
- **a)** $a^4 \times a^3$ a^7 (1 mark)
- **b)** $b^6 \div b^2$ b^4 (1 mark)

3 Simplify each of the following into one term.
- **a)** $2a + 3b + 1 - 6b + a + 5$ $3a$ $3a - 3b + b$ (1 mark)
- **b)** $4 - 4c + 3 - 3c + c$ $7 - 7c$ $7 - 6c$ (1 mark)

4 Multiply out the brackets.
- **a)** $3(2x + 3y + z)$ $6x + 9y + 3z$ (1 mark)
- **b)** $-2x(x^3 - y^2)$ (1 mark)

5 Multiply out the brackets and simplify.
- **a)** $2(a - 1) + 3(3a + 4)$ $11a + 10$ (1 mark)
- **b)** $5(x + 3) - 2(x - 2)$ $3x + 19$ (1 mark)

Score /10

Answer all parts of the questions. Use a separate sheet of paper if necessary.

1 These are statements about values of p.

Tick those that are true.

The first row has been completed.

Statement	$p = 3$	$p = 4$	$p = 5$	$p = 7$
p is greater than 4			✓	✓
$3p$ is equal to 12		✓		
$3 + p$ is less than 7	✓			
p^2 is greater than 20			✓	✓

(2 marks)

2 a) Complete this table about values of n.

n	$n + 2$	$2n - 3$
2	4	1
3	5	3
5	7	7

(2 marks)

b) Write down two possible operations to complete this table.

n	$n \div 6$	$n - 30$
36	6	6

(1 mark)

3 Three of these expressions are equal. Circle the two that are not equal.

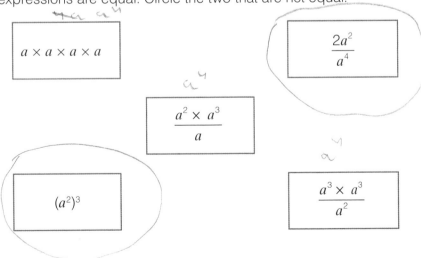

$a \times a \times a \times a$

$\dfrac{2a^2}{a^4}$

$\dfrac{a^2 \times a^3}{a}$

$(a^2)^3$

$\dfrac{a^3 \times a^3}{a^2}$

(1 mark)

Score   /6

For more help on this topic see KS3 Maths Revision Guide pages 20–21.

A Choose just one answer, a, b, c or d.

1 Which of these equals
$4m + 3n - 7$? (1 mark)
a) $2m + 1 + 4n - 2m + n + 6$ ☐
b) $2m - 1 + 4n + 2m - n - 6$ ☐
c) $2m - 1 + 4n - 2m + n - 6$ ☐
d) $2m + 1 - 4n + 2m - n + 6$ ☑

2 Which is the common factor of
$6y^2 - 4y$? (1 mark)
a) $2y^2$ ☐ b) y^2 ☐
c) 2 ☐ d) $2y$ ☐

3 Which pair of brackets equals
$5c^2 + 13c - 6$? (1 mark)
a) $(c + 3)(5c - 2)$ ☑
b) $(5c + 3)(c + 2)$ ☐
c) $(5c - 3)(c - 2)$ ☐
d) $(c - 3)(5c + 2)$ ☐

4 Which expression comes from
$(4 - 3b)(3 - b)$? (1 mark)
a) $12 + 13b - 3b^2$ ☐
b) $12 + 13b + 3b^2$ ☐
c) $3b^2 - 13b + 12$ ☐
d) $3b^2 + 13b - 12$ ☐

5 Which of these is the difference of
two squares? (1 mark)
a) $16 + 4x^2$ ☐
b) $25 - 5y^2$ ☐
c) $n^2 - 4$ ☐
d) $b^2 - 24$ ☑

Score /5

B Answer all parts of each question.

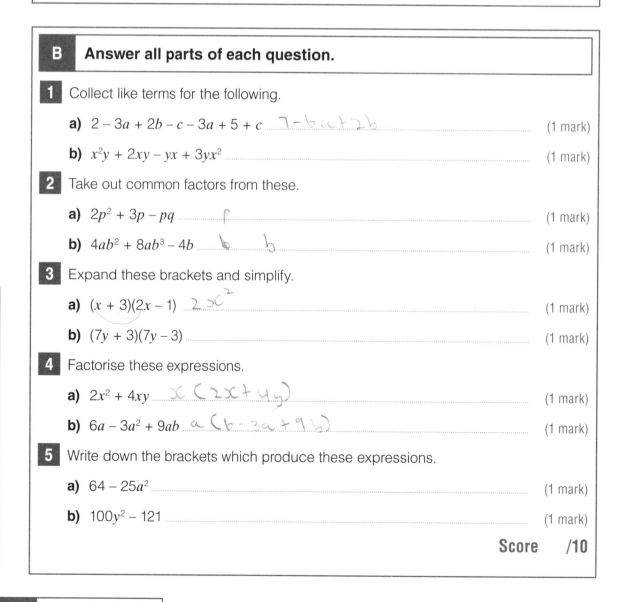

1 Collect like terms for the following.

a) $2 - 3a + 2b - c - 3a + 5 + c$ $7 - 6a + 2b$ (1 mark)

b) $x^2y + 2xy - yx + 3yx^2$ (1 mark)

2 Take out common factors from these.

a) $2p^2 + 3p - pq$ p (1 mark)

b) $4ab^2 + 8ab^3 - 4b$ b b (1 mark)

3 Expand these brackets and simplify.

a) $(x + 3)(2x - 1)$ $2x^2$ (1 mark)

b) $(7y + 3)(7y - 3)$ (1 mark)

4 Factorise these expressions.

a) $2x^2 + 4xy$ $x(2x + 4y)$ (1 mark)

b) $6a - 3a^2 + 9ab$ $a(b - 3a + 9b)$ (1 mark)

5 Write down the brackets which produce these expressions.

a) $64 - 25a^2$ (1 mark)

b) $100y^2 - 121$ (1 mark)

Score /10

C   **Answer all parts of the questions. Use a separate sheet of paper if necessary.**

1   **a)**   Circle the expression below that is the same as $a^2 + 6a + 8$.

$(a + 3)(a + 1)$ $(a + 4)(a + 2)$

$(a + 1)(a + 2)$

$(a + 5)(a + 3)$ $(a + 1)(a + 8)$

(1 mark)

   b)   Prove that the sum of two of the above expressions, multiplied out, can be simplified to make:

$$2a^2 + 11a + 17$$

(1 mark)

2   Two expressions are written on cards.

$5a - 3$ $3a - 7$

What value of a makes the expressions equal?

Show all your working.

(1 mark)

3   A rectangle has dimensions $3a$ by $7b$.

$3a$

$7b$

Write down an expression in its simplest terms for the following.

a)   Area of rectangle (A)

(1 mark)

b)   Perimeter of rectangle (P)

(1 mark)

Score   /5

For more help on this topic see KS3 Maths Revision Guide pages 22–23.

A   **Choose just one answer, a, b, c or d.**

1 Which is the rule for 'Think of a number, double it and find a third'? (1 mark)

a) $\dfrac{2n}{3}$ ☐   b) $\dfrac{3n}{2}$ ☐

c) $\dfrac{(n+3)}{3}$ ☐   d) $\dfrac{(n+2)}{2}$ ☐

2 If $A = \dfrac{1}{2}(a + b)h$, which is A when $a = 3$, $b = 4$ and $h = 5$? (1 mark)

a) 20 ☐   b) 17.5 ☐

c) 13.5 ☐   d) 35 ☐

3 If $F = \dfrac{9C}{5} + 32$, which of these gives C? (1 mark)

a) $C = \dfrac{5F}{9} - 32$ ☐

b) $C = 32 - \dfrac{9F}{5}$ ☐

c) $C = \dfrac{5F - 160}{9}$ ☐

d) $C = \dfrac{32 - 9F}{5}$ ☐

4 Find V in terms of π if $r = 3.2$ in the formula $V = \dfrac{4}{3}\pi r^3$. (1 mark)

a) $V = 12.8\pi$ ☐

b) $V = 4.27\pi$ ☐

c) $V = 43.69\pi$ ☐

d) $V = 13.65\pi$ ☐

5 If $\dfrac{a}{\sin A} = \dfrac{b}{\sin B}$, which of these gives a? (1 mark)

a) $a = b \times \sin A \times \sin B$ ☐

b) $a = b(\sin A + \sin B)$ ☐

c) $a = \dfrac{\sin A}{b \sin B}$ ☐

d) $a = \dfrac{b \sin A}{\sin B}$ ☐

Score   /5

B   **Answer all parts of each question.**

1 An apple costs Ap and a banana costs Bp. What is the formula for the cost of:

a) 5 apples and 3 bananas? .... (1 mark)

b) 8 apples and 6 bananas? .... (1 mark)

2 The formula for the volume of a cuboid is $V = lwh$. Find the volume when:

a) l = 6cm, w = 4.5cm, h = 5cm .... (1 mark)

b) l = 42mm, w = 18mm, h = 27mm .... (1 mark)

3 Change the subject of the formula to h.

a) $V = \dfrac{1}{3}\pi r^2 h$ .... (1 mark)

b) $SA = 2\pi rh + 2\pi r^2$ .... (1 mark)

4 $A = bh$ gives the area of a parallelogram. If $A = 64\text{cm}^2$ and $b = 2h$:

a) Find h to 2 d.p. .... (1 mark)

b) Find b to 2 d.p. .... (1 mark)

5 Use $F = \dfrac{9C}{5} + 32$ to convert the following to the other scale (to 1 d.p.).

a) 18°C .... (1 mark)

b) 72°F .... (1 mark)

Score   /10

C Answer all parts of the questions. Use a separate sheet of paper if necessary.

1 A class is set the following puzzle:

> **Think of a number, square it, divide by 4 and subtract 1.**

a) Write down a rule for any number n.

(1 mark)

b) What value of n gives the result zero? Show all your working.

(1 mark)

2 The formula $I = PRT$ works out the interest (I) paid on an amount (P) at an annual rate (R) for T years. 🖩

a) What would the formula be if the rate of interest needed to be found? Show all your working.

(1 mark)

b) What is the interest earned on £6500, invested for five years at a fixed annual rate of 2.5%? Show all your working.

£.. (1 mark)

c) A sum of money has been invested at 3% for five years.

The amount of interest earned is £1350. How much was invested? Show all your working.

£.. (1 mark)

3 A father is twice as tall as his son. His son has an older sister, who is 5cm taller than him, and a younger sister, who is 2cm shorter than him. The son's height is $h$cm.

a) Write down an expression in h for:

i) the height of the father

(1 mark)

ii) the height of the older sister

(1 mark)

iii) the height of the younger sister

(1 mark)

b) If the height of the father is 180cm, work out the heights of the three children.

(2 marks)

Score   /10

For more help on this topic see KS3 Maths Revision Guide pages 24–25.

A Choose just one answer, a, b, c or d, giving the correct solution for each equation.

1 $4m = 96$ (1 mark)
a) $m = 24$
b) $m = 23$
c) $m = 14$
d) $m = 16$

4 $2q + 7 = 13 - q$ (1 mark)
a) $q = 7$
b) $q = 6$
c) $q = 3$
d) $q = 2$

2 $2n - 3 = 15$ (1 mark)
a) $n = 7.5$
b) $n = 18$
c) $n = 9$
d) $n = 6$

5 $5(r + 2) = 3(2r - 3)$ (1 mark)
a) $r = 19$
b) $r = 10$
c) $r = 1$
d) $r = 2$

Score /5

3 $\dfrac{3p}{4} = -5$ (1 mark)

a) $p = -6\frac{2}{3}$

b) $p = 6\frac{3}{4}$

c) $p = 6\frac{3}{5}$

d) $p = -5\frac{3}{4}$

B Solve each of the following equations.

1 a) $6a = -78$ (1 mark)

b) $7b = 53$ (1 mark)

2 a) $4 + 3a = 19$ (1 mark)

b) $21 = 2b - 3$ (1 mark)

3 a) $\dfrac{5a}{8} = 3$ (1 mark)

b) $\dfrac{b}{12} = -\dfrac{1}{6}$ (1 mark)

4 a) $4a - 7 = 3a + 4$ (1 mark)

b) $5 + 2b = 7 - 5b$ (1 mark)

5 a) $3(2a + 1) = 10$ (1 mark)

b) $3(2 - b) - 4(2 - 3b) = 16$ (1 mark)

Score /10

EQUATIONS

MODULE 11

1 **a)** This square and rectangle have the same area:

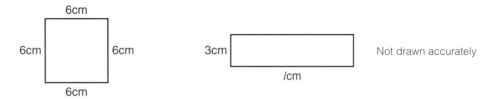

6cm

6cm   6cm

6cm

3cm

$l$cm

Not drawn accurately

Work out the value of l.

Show all your working.

.... cm   (1 mark)

b) This triangle and rectangle have the same area:

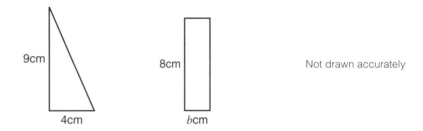

9cm

4cm

8cm

$b$cm

Not drawn accurately

Work out the value of b.

Show all your working.

.... cm   (2 marks)

2 This is a quadrilateral:

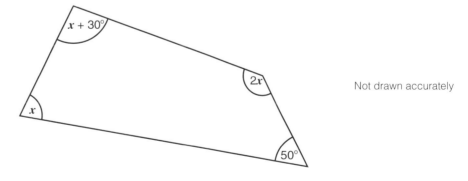

$x + 30°$

$2x$

x

$50°$

Not drawn accurately

a) Write down an equation for the sum of the angles in the quadrilateral in terms of x.

(1 mark)

b) Solve the equation to find the three unknown angles of the quadrilateral.

(2 marks)

Score   /6

For more help on this topic see KS3 Maths Revision Guide pages 26–27.

A · Choose just one answer, a, b, c or d.

1 On a graph, which are the coordinates of the origin? (1 mark)
   a) (0, 1)
   b) (0, 0)
   c) (1, 0)
   d) (1, 1)

2 In which quadrant is the point (−3, −1)? (1 mark)
   a) 1st
   b) 2nd
   c) 3rd
   d) 4th

3 The line $x = 0$ is: (1 mark)
   a) sloping 'upwards'
   b) sloping 'downwards'
   c) vertical
   d) horizontal

4 A square (side 4 units) is drawn so its centre is the origin. Which of these points is a vertex? (1 mark)
   a) (1, 1)
   b) (−1, 2)
   c) (2, −1)
   d) (2, −2)

5 Which of these points is another vertex of the square in question 4? (1 mark)
   a) (−2, −2)
   b) (−1, −1)
   c) (1, 2)
   d) (2, −1)

Score /5

B · On graph paper, draw an x-axis and a y-axis. Label both axes so that $−4 \leqslant x \leqslant +4$ and $−4 \leqslant y \leqslant +4$.

Use it to answer all parts of each question.

1
   a) Plot points A(2, 2) and C(1, 3). (1 mark)

   b) Draw a square $ABCD$ so that AC is the diagonal. (1 mark)

   c) What are the coordinates of B and D? .... (1 mark)

2 The square in question 1 is moved horizontally so that A becomes the point A'(−1, 2).

Give the new coordinates of:

B' .... C' .... D' .... (1 mark)

3 The square in question 1 is moved twice more. First, A becomes the point A''(−1, −2). Then A is moved again to become A'''(2, −2).

Give the new coordinates of:

   a) B'' .... C'' .... D'' .... (1 mark)

   b) B''' .... C''' .... D''' .... (1 mark)

Score /6

Answer all parts of the questions. Use a separate sheet of paper if necessary.

1 Use graph paper for this question.

a) Plot the points $J(2, 0)$, $K(0, 2)$, $L(-2, 0)$, $M(0, -2)$.

b) Join $J \rightarrow K \rightarrow L \rightarrow M \rightarrow J$.

c) Join the midpoints of JK, KL, LM, MJ to form the square $PQRS$.

d) Write the equation of the line RS.

(3 marks)

e) Is $y = x$ the equation of the straight line through Q and S?

Tick (✓) Yes or No

☐ Yes   ☐ No

Explain your answer.

(1 mark)

2 P and Q are fixed. The x-coordinate of R cannot change but the y-coordinate of R can change.

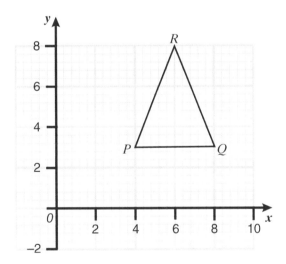

Triangle PQR is isosceles when R is at the point $(6, 8)$.

a) Give the coordinates of another point R where triangle PQR is still isosceles.

(1 mark)

b) Give the two possible sets of coordinates of a point R where triangle PQR is an equilateral triangle. Give your answers to 1 decimal place where necessary.

(2 marks)

Score   /7

For more help on this topic see KS3 Maths Revision Guide pages 28–29.

A **Choose just one answer, a, b, c or d.**

1 Which equation produces a
straight line? *(1 mark)*
a) $y = 3x + 1$ ☐
b) $y = 3x^2 + x + 1$ ☐
c) $2y - x^3 = 3$ ☐
d) $x^2 + y^2 = 1$ ☐

2 Which equation produces
a parabola? *(1 mark)*
a) $y = 3x - 2$ ☐
b) $x + y = 4$ ☐
c) $y = 3x^2 - 2$ ☐
d) $y = \dfrac{3}{x}$ ☐

3 What is the name of the function
$y = 2x^3 + 3x + 4$? *(1 mark)*
a) reciprocal ☐ b) cubic ☐
c) linear ☐ d) exponential ☐

4 On the line $y = 2x - 1$, what is the
y-coordinate $(4, y)$? *(1 mark)*
a) 8 ☐ b) 7 ☐
c) −7 ☐ d) 1 ☐

5 On the curve $2y = x^3 - 2$, what is the
y-coordinate $(-2, y)$? *(1 mark)*
a) 3 ☐ b) 6 ☐
c) −10 ☐ d) −5 ☐

Score /5

B **Work out a table of coordinates for each of these functions
using −2 ≤ x ≤ +2, giving your answers to 1 d.p. where necessary.**

1 $y = 5x - 2$

x	−2	−1	0	1	2
y					

(1 mark)

2 $y = 2x^2 - 3$

x	−2	−1	0	1	2
y					

(1 mark)

3 $y = 3 - x^3$

x	−2	−1	0	1	2
y					

(1 mark)

4 $y = 3^x$

x	−2	−1	0	1	2
y					

(1 mark)

5 For this function, use −3 ≤ x < 0 and 0 < x ≤ +3.

$y = \dfrac{5}{x}$

x	−3	−2	−1	1	2	3
y						

(1 mark)

Score /5

C   **Answer all parts of the questions. Use a separate sheet of paper if necessary.**

1 These are the equations of five straight lines.

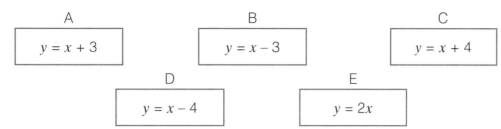

A
$y = x + 3$

B
$y = x - 3$

C
$y = x + 4$

D
$y = x - 4$

E
$y = 2x$

a) Do any of these lines go through (0, 0)?

Tick (✓)   ☐ A   ☐ B   ☐ C   ☐ D   ☐ E

Explain your answer.

(1 mark)

Do not use the point (0, 0) for parts **b)** and **c)**.

b) Complete this sentence with the letter of the line, A, B, C, D or E, and the missing coordinate.

Straight line .... goes through point (0, ...).

(1 mark)

c) Complete this sentence with the letter of the line, A, B, C, D or E, and the missing coordinate.

Straight line .... goes through point (................., 0).

(1 mark)

2 Match each of these graphs to the correct equation.

Graph .... illustrates
the equation $y = 3x - 4$

Graph .... illustrates
the equation $y = 5x^3$

Graph .... illustrates
the equation $y = 4 - x$

Graph .... illustrates
the equation $y = x^2 - 3$

Graph .... illustrates
the equation $y = \frac{1}{4x}$

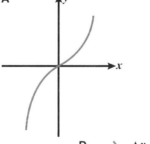
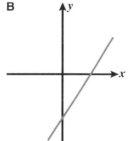
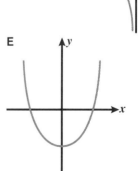

(2 marks)

Score   /5

For more help on this topic see KS3 Maths Revision Guide pages 30–31.

A Choose just one answer, a, b, c or d.

1 The general equation of a straight line is: (1 mark)
a) $y = mx - c$
b) $y = cx + m$
c) $y = mx + c$
d) $y = cx - m$

2 Intercept (c) is the point where the line crosses: (1 mark)
a) the y-axis
b) the x-axis
c) the origin
d) another line

3 A line with gradient = +3 is: (1 mark)
a) parallel with y-axis
b) parallel with x-axis
c) going 'uphill' (from left to right)
d) going 'downhill' (from left to right)

4 The gradient of the line $2y = 4x + 1$ is: (1 mark)
a) 4
b) 2
c) −4
d) −2

5 The y-intercept of the line $3y = 2x - 9$ is: (1 mark)
a) −3
b) −9
c) 2
d) 3

Score /5

B Answer all the parts of each question.

1 Write down the gradient and y-intercept of:
a) $x + 4y = 3$ (1 mark)
b) $\frac{y}{2} = x - 4$ (1 mark)

2 Sketch the lines with these gradients and y-intercepts.
a) $m = 2, c = 3$ (1 mark)
b) $m = -1, c = 5$ (1 mark)

3 Are these lines going 'uphill' or 'downhill' (from left to right)?
a) $2x - y = 3$ (1 mark)
b) $y = 1 - 4x$ (1 mark)

4 Work out the equation of these lines.
a) gradient = −3; line passes through (0, 4) (1 mark)
b) gradient = $+\frac{1}{2}$; line passes through (1, 3) (1 mark)

Score /8

C   **Answer all parts of the questions. Use a separate sheet of paper if necessary.**

1   **a)**   Sketch a line that has equal positive x and positive y-intercepts.

(1 mark)

   b)   Prove that the value of the gradient will always be the same.

(1 mark)

   c)   What is the value of the gradient?

(1 mark)

2   A line goes through the points A(0, –1) and B(10, 4).

Draw this line on graph paper.

   a)   Work out the gradient of this line from the graph.

Show all extra lines drawn.

(1 mark)

   b)   Write down the equation of the line going through A and B.

(1 mark)

   c)   Draw another line that is parallel to AB.

Work out its gradient.

(2 marks)

   d)   Complete this sentence.

Parallel lines have gradients that are ....

(1 mark)

3   **a)**   Plot the points (4, –3) and (9, 7) on graph paper and draw a line through them.

(1 mark)

   b)   Work out the gradient of the line and write down the y-intercept.

(1 mark)

   c)   Write down the equation of the line.

(1 mark)

Score   /11

For more help on this topic see KS3 Maths Revision Guide pages 32–33.

A	**Choose just one answer, a, b, c or d.**

1 Which point lies on line
$y = x + 3$? (1 mark)
a) (4, –1) ☐
b) (8, –2) ☐
c) (–4, –1) ☐
d) (–2, 8) ☐

4 Which line has a negative
gradient? (1 mark)
a) $2y - x = 1$ ☐
b) $2y + 3 = x$ ☐
c) $y = 4x - 1$ ☐
d) $y = 6 - 5x$ ☐

2 Which point lies on line
$y = x^2 - 1$? (1 mark)
a) (–3, 4) ☐
b) (3, 8) ☐
c) (–2, 4) ☐
d) (2, 8) ☐

5 Which is a point where $y = x^2 - 2x$
crosses the x-axis? (1 mark)
a) (2, 0) ☐
b) (0, 2) ☐
c) (1, 0) ☐
d) (0, –1) ☐

Score /5

3 How many solutions of a quadratic
equation can be found by drawing
its graph? (1 mark)
a) 2 ☐
b) 1 ☐
c) 3 ☐
d) 4 ☐

B	**Answer each of these questions using graph paper.**
	Work out a table of coordinates for each function and draw its graph.

1 Solve the equations

$y = 7 - x$

$y = x + 1$

.... (2 marks)

2 Write down the coordinates of the point of intersection of these graphs.

$y = x^2 - 3x + 1$

$y = 1 - x$

.... (2 marks)

3 Solve the equation by finding the x-coordinates where $y = 0$.

$y = x^2 - 6x + 5$

.... (2 marks)

Score /6

1 The local cinema charges more for adults than for children.

Two families go to see a film.

Mr & Mrs A take two children. They pay a total of £24.80

Mrs B takes three children. She pays a total of £23.20

By forming two equations, work out the cost of a child ticket and an adult ticket. Show all your working.

one child: £..

one adult: £.. (2 marks)

2 These two lines meet at the point (a, b):

$$y = 2x + 3 \qquad\qquad 2y = 4 - x$$

a) Work out the tables of coordinates and draw the graphs of the two lines to find the values of a and b.

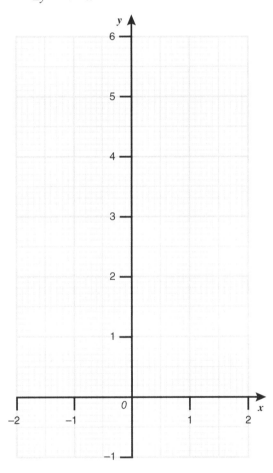

$a =$ .... $b =$ ....

(3 marks)

b) What does the point (a, b) tell you?

(1 mark)

Score /6

For more help on this topic see KS3 Maths Revision Guide pages 34–35.

A Choose just one answer, a, b, c or d, giving the correct answers about this travel graph of a vehicle's journey.

1 How many times does the vehicle stop? (1 mark)
- **a)** 0 ☐ **b)** 1 ☐
- **c)** 2 ☐ **d)** 3 ☐

2 How far does the vehicle travel? (1 mark)
- **a)** 5km ☐ **b)** 4km ☐
- **c)** 6km ☐ **d)** 3km ☐

3 When is the fastest part of the journey? (1 mark)
- **a)** 25–30 minutes ☐
- **b)** 40–50 minutes ☐
- **c)** 0–10 minutes ☐
- **d)** 15–20 minutes ☐

4 How many minutes is the longest stop? (1 mark)
- **a)** 10 minutes ☐
- **b)** 15 minutes ☐
- **c)** 20 minutes ☐
- **d)** 5 minutes ☐

5 How long does the journey take? (1 mark)
- **a)** 40 minutes ☐
- **b)** 50 minutes ☐
- **c)** 1 hour 10 minutes ☐
- **d)** 1 hour 40 minutes ☐

Score /5

B Answer all parts of the question.

1 Sketch a graph to illustrate the following.

a) A car travelling at constant speed; show speed against time (1 mark)

b) Converting £ to $ (1 mark)

c) Water being poured into a test-tube; show depth against time (1 mark)

d) The area of a circle as the radius increases (1 mark)

Score /4

Answer all parts of the questions. Use a separate sheet of paper if necessary.

1 The graph shows how the sales of Slurp ice cream have changed over three years.

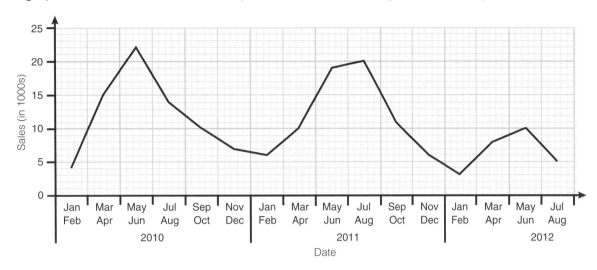

a) The sales of ice cream were at their lowest in January 2012.

When were the sales of ice cream at their highest?

(1 mark)

b) At what time of year were ice cream sales at their lowest in each year? Explain why this might be.

(2 marks)

2 This graph illustrates a cycle ride.

a) What happened at 9 miles?

(1 mark)

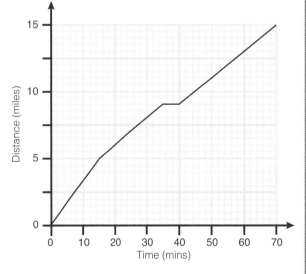

b) At what speed did the cyclist start the journey?

Show all your working.

.... mph   (2 marks)

c) How long did the whole journey take?

(1 mark)

d) What was the average speed for the whole journey?

Show all your working.

.... mph   (2 marks)

Score   /9

For more help on this topic see KS3 Maths Revision Guide pages 36–37.

A | Choose just one answer, a, b, c or d, giving the next two terms in each sequence.

1 5, 8, 11, 14, _, _,... (1 mark)
a) 15, 16 ☐
b) 16, 18 ☐
c) 17, 20 ☐
d) 16, 19 ☐

2 98, 93, 88, 83, _, _,... (1 mark)
a) 84, 85 ☐
b) 78, 73 ☐
c) 73, 68 ☐
d) 78, 77 ☐

3 4, 12, 36, 108, _, _,... (1 mark)
a) 210, 312 ☐
b) 324, 972 ☐
c) 216, 432 ☐
d) 200, 300 ☐

4 3125, 625, 125, 25, _, _,... (1 mark)
a) 5, 1 ☐
b) 20, 15 ☐
c) 20, 10 ☐
d) 15, 5 ☐

5 144, 121, 100, 81, _, _,... (1 mark)
a) 96, 84 ☐
b) 90, 71 ☐
c) 64, 49 ☐
d) 70, 60 ☐

Score /5

B | Answer all parts of each question.

1 Find the 20th term in the sequences with these nth terms.

a) $3n + 4$ .... (1 mark)

b) $n(n + 2)$ .... (1 mark)

2 Find the nth term of these sequences.

a) 3, 6, 9, 12, 15, … .... (1 mark)

b) 7, 12, 17, 22, … .... (1 mark)

3 Find the next three terms of these sequences.

a) 3, 6, 11, 18, _, _, _,... .... (1 mark)

b) 46 875, 9375, 1875, 375, _, _, _,... .... (1 mark)

4 a) Write down the rule for this sequence.

1, 16, 81, 256,... .... (1 mark)

b) Find its nth term. .... (1 mark)

Score /8

Answer all parts of the questions. Use a separate sheet of paper if necessary.

1 This table shows information about three different sequences, P, Q and R.

Write in the missing information.

	1st term	2nd term	3rd term	4th term	nth term
Sequence P	28	26	24	22	$30 - 2n$
Sequence Q	28	24	20	16	$32 -$
Sequence R	28				$34 - 6n$

(2 marks)

2 These patterns are made up of shaded and unshaded squares.

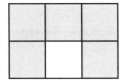

Pattern 1

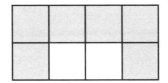

Pattern 2

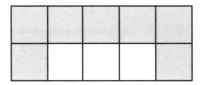

Pattern 3

a) Draw the next two patterns.

(1 mark)

b) Imagine a pattern with n unshaded squares.

Write an expression for the squares in a ratio of unshaded : shaded.

(1 mark)

c) How many shaded squares are in the 10th pattern?

(1 mark)

3 The nth term of a sequence is $n^3 - 1$. Work out the values of the following terms. ▦

a) Term 4

(1 mark)

b) Term 7

(1 mark)

c) Term 25

(1 mark)

Score /8

For more help on this topic see KS3 Maths Revision Guide pages 38–39.

A Choose just one answer, a, b, c or d.

1 How many centimetres in 1km? *(1 mark)*
- **a)** 100cm
- **b)** 1000cm
- **c)** 100000cm
- **d)** 1000000cm

2 How many milligrams in 2.5kg? *(1 mark)*
- **a)** 2500mg
- **b)** 25000mg
- **c)** 2500000mg
- **d)** 25000000mg

3 How many litres in 5 gallons? *(1 mark)*
- **a)** 22.5*l*
- **b)** 20*l*
- **c)** 22*l*
- **d)** 20.5*l*

4 How long is it from 10.15am to 1.30pm? *(1 mark)*
- **a)** 3 hours
- **b)** 3 hours 15 minutes
- **c)** 2 hours 30 minutes
- **d)** 2 hours

5 What is the time taken to travel 6 miles at 30mph? *(1 mark)*
- **a)** 10 minutes
- **b)** 12 minutes
- **c)** 20 minutes
- **d)** 30 minutes

Score /5

B Answer all parts of each question.

1 Calculate the average speed for these journeys.

a) Distance = 55km, time taken = 40 minutes. Give your answer in km/h.

.... *(1 mark)*

b) Distance = 250 miles, time taken = 4 hours. Give your answer in mph.

.... *(1 mark)*

2 A train leaves Manchester at 11:05 and arrives in London at 13:12.

a) What are the times in the 12-hour clock?

.... *(1 mark)*

b) How long did the journey take?

.... *(1 mark)*

3 A container holds 2.5 litres of water.

a) How many centilitres of water does the container hold?

.... *(1 mark)*

b) How many pints of water does the container hold? Give your answer to 1 d.p.

.... *(1 mark)*

Score /6

Answer all parts of the questions. Use a separate sheet of paper if necessary.

1 This table shows the times of low tides at Hull (Albert Dock) during the first week of December.

December	1	2	3	4	5	6	7
1st low tide	11:03	11:54	00:16	01:06	01:54	02:40	03:26
2nd low tide	23:24	–	12:42	13:28	14:12	14:54	15:36

a) Which day had only one low tide?

(1 mark)

b) When was there a low tide at 16 minutes past midnight?

(1 mark)

c) Which day had the longest time between the two low tides?

(1 mark)

2 Circle the most likely measurement for each of the following.

a) A coffee mug holds about:

200ml

300ml

400ml

$\frac{1}{2}$ litre

(1 mark)

b) A mobile phone weighs about:

125 seconds

125ml

125g

125 minutes

(1 mark)

c) The height of an apple tree is about:

4km

4m

4cm

4mm

(1 mark)

Score   /6

For more help on this topic see KS3 Maths Revision Guide pages 42–43.

A Choose just one answer, a, b, c or d.

1 The actual distance of 5.5cm using a scale of 1 : 30 is: (1 mark)
a) 15cm ☐   b) 100cm ☐
c) 150cm ☐   d) 165cm ☐

2 The scaled distance of 4.2km using a scale of 1 : 125 is: (1 mark)
a) 336 000cm ☐
b) 33 600cm ☐
c) 3360cm ☐
d) 336cm ☐

3 A map, drawn to scale 1 : 1 000 000, shows towns A and B. Their actual distance apart is 63km. What is the map distance? (1 mark)
a) 6.3cm ☐   b) 63cm ☐
c) 60cm ☐   d) 6cm ☐

4 A model, built to scale 1 : 50, has a height of 16cm. What is its actual height? (1 mark)
a) 800mm ☐
b) 800cm ☐
c) 160cm ☐
d) 1.6m ☐

5 What is the angle between N and SE? (1 mark)
a) 100° ☐
b) 270° ☐
c) 180° ☐
d) 135° ☐

Score   /5

B Answer all parts of each question.

1 These lines are drawn to scale 1 : 20. What are their actual lengths?
a) _____ .... cm (1 mark)
b) _____ .... cm (1 mark)

2 This is a sketch of a journey from A to B.

N, B, 62°, 5.6cm, A

a) If the scale is 1 : 1 500 000, what is the actual distance from A to B in km? (1 mark)

b) What is the bearing of B from A? (1 mark)

3 Draw these lines using a scale of 1 : 20
a) 96cm (1 mark)
b) 260mm (1 mark)

Score   /6

C   **Answer all parts of the questions. Use a separate sheet of paper if necessary.**

1   A bird flies 6km, on a bearing of 084°, from a wall (W) to a tree (T).

It then flies 4.5km, on a bearing of 230°, to its nest (B).

a)   Draw a scale diagram to illustrate the bird's journey. Use a scale of 1cm = 1km

(2 marks)

b)   What is the distance and bearing of the bird's nest from the original wall?

Distance: .... km

Bearing: .... °   (1 mark)

2   **a)**   On a map of a golf course, the distance from the tee to the eighteenth hole measures 13cm.

The scale is given as 1cm to 20m.

How far is the distance on the actual course?

Show all your working.

.... m   (1 mark)

b)   The actual distance of the tee to the first hole is 210m.

What is the distance on the map?

Show all your working.

.... cm   (1 mark)

Score   /5

For more help on this topic see KS3 Maths Revision Guide pages 44–45.

A — Choose just one answer, a, b, c or d.

1 What fraction of an hour is 35 minutes? (1 mark)

a) $\frac{6}{12}$ ☐ b) $\frac{6}{7}$ ☐

c) $\frac{7}{12}$ ☐ d) $\frac{5}{12}$ ☐

2 What % of £96 is £12? (1 mark)

a) 12.5% ☐ b) 10% ☐

c) 20% ☐ d) 25% ☐

3 What fraction of 2kg is 400g? (1 mark)

a) $\frac{4}{25}$ ☐ b) $\frac{3}{20}$ ☐

c) $\frac{2}{5}$ ☐ d) $\frac{1}{5}$ ☐

4 What % of a year is 1 week? (1 mark)

a) 1.923% ☐
b) 2.8% ☐
c) 2.55% ☐
d) 5.2% ☐

5 What fraction of 1 week is a weekend? (1 mark)

a) $\frac{4}{7}$ ☐ b) $\frac{3}{7}$ ☐

c) $\frac{2}{7}$ ☐ d) $\frac{1}{7}$ ☐

Score /5

B — Answer all parts of each question.

1 Some houses on two roads have double-glazed windows.

Work out the fraction of houses with double-glazed windows on each road.

a) 62 out of 104 houses on the first road have double-glazed windows. (1 mark)

b) 84 out of 120 houses on the second road have double-glazed windows. (1 mark)

2 Work out the percentage (to the nearest whole number) of aisle seats in two cinemas.

a) 120 aisle seats out of a total of 660 seats in the first cinema. (1 mark)

b) 120 aisle seats out of a total of 572 seats in the second cinema. (1 mark)

3 A man has six weeks of holiday a year.

a) What fraction of the year does he work? (1 mark)

b) What percentage of the year is he on holiday? (1 mark)

Score /6

Answer all parts of the questions. Use a separate sheet of paper if necessary.

1 **a)** Three-fifths of the members of a swimming club are female.

Five-twelfths of these females are over 20 years old.

What fraction of the members of the club are females over 20 years old?

Show all your working.

(1 mark)

b) The club has 80 members. How many are male?

Show all your working.

(1 mark)

c) Fifty per cent of the males at the club are over 20 years old.

What fraction of the total club membership is over 20 years old?

Show all your working.

(1 mark)

2 In one shop, Smarts, a TV costs £599.99 after a discount of £100, but exclusive of VAT at 20%.

Another shop, Wises, is selling the same TV for £699.99. There is no discount but VAT is included.

Smarts	**Wises**

Discount price: £599.99 (excluding VAT)	£699.99 (including VAT)

Which is the better buy?

Show all your working. 🖩

(2 marks)

Score **/5**

For more help on this topic see KS3 Maths Revision Guide pages 46–47.

A Choose just one answer, a, b, c or d.

1 16 : 24 simplified is: (1 mark)
- **a)** 2 : 3 ☐
- **b)** 8 : 16 ☐
- **c)** 4 : 8 ☐
- **d)** 1 : 2 ☐

2 10 : 15 : 35 simplified is: (1 mark)
- **a)** 2 : 3 : 5 ☐
- **b)** 5 : 3 : 6 ☐
- **c)** 2 : 3 : 7 ☐
- **d)** 1 : 2 : 3 ☐

3 What is 24 hours divided into the ratio 3 : 4 : 5? (1 mark)
- **a)** 11 hours : 10 hours : 3 hours ☐
- **b)** 12 hours : 3 hours : 9 hours ☐
- **c)** 10 hours : 5 hours : 9 hours ☐
- **d)** 6 hours : 8 hours : 10 hours ☐

4 A coffee drink is made from coffee and milk in the ratio 3 : 2. How much milk is in 350ml of the drink? (1 mark)
- **a)** 150ml ☐
- **b)** 140ml ☐
- **c)** 200ml ☐
- **d)** 250ml ☐

5 What fraction of the drink in question 4 is coffee? (1 mark)
- **a)** $\frac{2}{5}$ ☐
- **b)** $\frac{3}{5}$ ☐
- **c)** $\frac{4}{5}$ ☐
- **d)** $\frac{1}{5}$ ☐

Score /5

B Answer all parts of each question.

1 Simplify these ratios to lowest terms. (2 marks)

   a) 14 : 63 : 49 .... **b)** 9 : 15 : 24 ....

2 Divide these quantities into the ratio 2 : 5 : 3 (2 marks)

   a) £460 .... **b)** 750ml ....

3 A pizza is divided between three people. The portions are $\frac{1}{2}$, $\frac{1}{3}$ and $\frac{1}{6}$.

   a) What is the ratio of the portions?

   .... (1 mark)

   b) The pizza cost £9. The people pay in proportion to their portions.

      How much did they each pay?

   .... (1 mark)

4 A fruit salad is made from 12 strawberries, 20 blueberries and 18 raspberries.

   a) What fraction of the fruit salad contains blueberries?

   .... (1 mark)

   b) What is the ratio of fruit in the fruit salad?

   .... (1 mark)

Score /8

Module 1: Place value and ordering (pages 4–5)

A

1. b **2.** d **3.** c **4.** a **5.** d

B

1. 7, 100, 90, $\frac{4}{100}$

2. 32.024, 32.04, 32.3, 32.4

3. 21.65m, 2162cm, 21 170mm, 20.25m, 2020cm

4. 3.65 > 3.43, 41.6 < 46.1, 87.204 > 87.02, 0.41 < 0.43

5. 0.42km ≠ 4300m, 87.204m = 8720.4cm,
363g = 0.363kg, £44.60 ≠ 4406p

C

1.

10p coins	20p coins
1	4
3	3
5	2
7	1
9	0

(2 marks for all correct; 1 mark if one row is incorrect)

2. a) 28 + 72 = 100 *(1 mark)*
b) 54 − 28 = 26 *(1 mark)*
c) 72 × 54 = 3888 *(1 mark)*

3. 0.96 *(1 mark)*, 0.56 *(1 mark)*

4. 7795, 7685, 7575, 7465, 7355, 7245, 7135
(2 marks for all correct; 1 mark for at least five correct combinations)

Module 2: Factors, multiples and primes (pages 6–7)

A

1. b **2.** c **3.** b **4.** d **5.** a

B

1. a) 5, 25, 40 **b)** 4, 14, 7

2. a) $2^2 \times 3^2$ **b)** $2^4 \times 3$
c) $2 \times 3 \times 7$ **d)** $2^4 \times 5$

3. a) i) LCM = 90 **ii)** LCM = 60
b) i) HCF = 8 **ii)** HCF = 16

4. a) 30 **b)** 18

C

1. a) 120, 112 *(1 mark)*
b) Yes, 160 ÷ 8 = 20 exactly *(1 mark)*

2. a) 3, all the rest are multiples of 3 *(1 mark)*
b) 5, all the rest are multiples of 5 *(1 mark)*
c) 2, only even prime *(1 mark)*

3. a) 1, 3, 9 *(1 mark)* **b)** 9 *(1 mark)* **c)** 54 *(1 mark)*

Module 3: Number operations (pages 8–9)

A

1. c **2.** a **3.** d **4.** b **5.** c

B

1. a) 1515 **b)** 404.8

2. a) 1161 **b)** 32

3. a) −5°C **b)** +12°C

4. a) $1\frac{1}{10}$kg **b)** $\frac{17}{20}$kg

5. a) $1\frac{2}{5}$ **b)** $8\frac{19}{27}$

C

1. 30, 3 *(1 mark)*; 4, 20 *(1 mark)*

2. a) 03:32 *(1 mark)* **b)** Tuesday 01:15 *(1 mark)*
c) Monday 20:15 *(1 mark)* **d)** Monday 17:15 *(1 mark)*

Module 4: Powers and roots (pages 10–11)

A

1. c **2.** b **3.** d **4.** a **5.** c

B

1. a) 7776 **b)** 1

2. a) $3 \times 3 \times 3 \times 3$
b) $5 \times 5 \times 5 \times 5 \times 5 \times 5$

3. a) 2.35×10^{-5} **b)** 1.763×10^8

4. a) $6p^5q^3$ **b)** abc^{-2}
c) $128x^{12}$ **d)** $32e^{10}$

C

1. Integers are k and $k + 1 \Rightarrow k^2 + (k + 1)^2$
$= k^2 + k^2 + 2k + 1$ which is odd *(1 mark)*

2. a) Jan–Jul 2011 *(1 mark)*
b) 2012 − 2011 $\Rightarrow$ 31 110 − 30 798 = 312 *(1 mark)*
$= 3.12 \times 10^2$ *(1 mark)*
c) Increase, assuming it follows the pattern of the previous two years *(1 mark)*

3. 32, 9, 18, 5, 15
(2 marks for all correct; 1 mark if one row is incorrect)

Module 5: Decimals, fractions and percentages (pages 12–13)

A

1. c **2.** b **3.** b **4.** a **5.** d

B

1. a) 0.625 **b)** 1.8

2. a) 56.25% **b)** 46.875%

3. a) $\frac{54}{125}$ **b)** $\frac{7}{50}$

4. a) 60% **b)** 30% **c)** 14.17% **d)** 5.4%

C

1. a) 125%, 300%, 120%
(2 marks for all correct; otherwise 1 mark)
b) $\frac{2}{3}$ *(1 mark)* **c)** $\frac{5}{2}$ or $2\frac{1}{2}$ *(1 mark)*

2. 0.21 × 0.27 = 5.7% *(1 mark)*

3. a) $\frac{15}{8}$ **b)** 0.69 *(1 mark)*

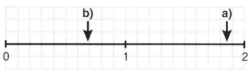

(1 mark)

Module 6: Approximations (pages 14–15)

A

1. c **2.** d **3.** a **4.** a **5.** d

B

1. a) 400 **b)** 1000

2. a) 0.0022 **b)** 11000

3. a) 2.322 **b)** 0.067

4. a) 30, 27.58 **b)** 0.72, 0.75
c) 16, 17.64 **d)** 11, 13.44

C

1. a) Broad Crag *(1 mark)* **b)** 3 *(1 mark)*
c) 1000 *(1 mark)*

2. a) 160 *(1 mark)*
b) adults: 80 × £18, children: 40 × £10,
students: 20 × £12, over 60s: 20 × £15 *(1 mark)*
total ticket sales = £1440 + £400 + £240 + £300 =
£2380 = £2400 to nearest £100 *(1 mark)*

Module 7: Calculator use (pages 16–17)

A

1. d **2.** a **3.** b **4.** b **5.** c

B

1. a) 13.203 **b)** 5.085

2. a) £3.40 **b)** 19.8kg

3. a) $\frac{10}{147}$ **b)** $2\frac{7}{24}$

4. a) 2.6×10^{-2} **b)** 3.72×10^5

5. a) 0.49 **b)** 7.29

C

1. a) 6 072 406 *(1 mark)*
b) $6.072 406 \times 10^6$ *(1 mark)*

2. a) 19.683 *(1 mark)*
b) 470 596 *(1 mark)*

ANSWERS

c) 4181.954 93 *(1 mark)*
d) 2.748 579 178 *(1 mark)*
3. b) 246 + 135 *(1 mark)*
c) 356 × 241 *(1 mark)*
d) 6534 ÷ 12 *(1 mark)*

ALGEBRA

Module 8: Notation and vocabulary (pages 18–19)

A
1. d 2. a 3. c 4. b 5. d

B
1. a) x^3y^2z b) $6a^3$
2. a) a^7 b) b^4
3. a) $3a - 3b + 6$ b) $7 - 6c$
4. a) $6x + 9y + 3z$ b) $-2x^4 + 2xy^2$
5. a) $11a + 10$ b) $3x + 19$

C
1.

Statement	$p = 3$	$p = 4$	$p = 5$	$p = 7$
p is greater than 4			✓	✓
$3p$ is equal to 12		✓		
$3 + p$ is less than 7	✓			
p^2 is greater than 20			✓	✓

(2 marks for all correct; 1 mark if one row is incorrect)

2. a)

n	$n + 2$	$2n - 3$
2	4	1
3	5	3
5	7	7

(2 marks for all correct; 1 mark if one row is incorrect)

b) $n \div 6$; $n - 30$; $\sqrt{n}$ *(1 mark)*
3. $(a^2)^3$, $\dfrac{2a^2}{a^4}$ *(1 mark)*

Module 9: Expressions (pages 20–21)

A
1. b 2. d 3. a 4. c 5. c

B
1. a) $7 - 6a + 2b$ b) $4x^2y + xy$
2. a) $p(2p + 3 - q)$ b) $4b(ab + 2ab^2 - 1)$
3. a) $2x^2 + 5x - 3$ b) $49y^2 - 9$
4. a) $2x(x + 2y)$ b) $3a(2 - a + 3b)$
5. a) $(8 - 5a)(8 + 5a)$ b) $(10y - 11)(10y + 11)$

C
1. a) $(a + 4)(a + 2)$ *(1 mark)*
   b) $(a + 5)(a + 3) + (a + 1)(a + 2) = a^2 + 8a + 15 + a^2 + 3a + 2$
   $= 2a^2 + 11a + 17$ *(1 mark)*
2. $5a - 3 = 3a - 7 \Rightarrow 2a = -4 \Rightarrow a = -2$ *(1 mark)*
3. a) $21ab$ *(1 mark)* b) $2(3a + 7b)$ or $6a + 14b$ *(1 mark)*

Module 10: Formulae (pages 22–23)

A
1. a 2. b 3. c 4. c 5. d

B
1. a) $5A + 3B$ b) $8A + 6B$
2. a) 135cm^3 b) $20\,412\text{mm}^3$ or 20.412cm^3
3. a) $h = \dfrac{3V}{\pi r^2}$ b) $h = \dfrac{SA - 2\pi r^2}{2\pi r}$
4. a) 5.66cm b) 11.31cm
5. a) 64.4°F b) 22.2°C

C
1. a) $\dfrac{n^2}{4} - 1$ *(1 mark)* b) 2 *(1 mark)*

2. a) $R = \dfrac{I}{PT}$ *(1 mark)*
   b) $I = 6500 \times 5 \times 0.025 = £812.50$ *(1 mark)*
   c) $P = \dfrac{I}{RT} \Rightarrow \dfrac{£1350}{0.03 \times 5} = £9000$ *(1 mark)*

3. a) i) $2h$cm *(1 mark)*
      ii) $(h + 5)$cm *(1 mark)*
      iii) $(h - 2)$cm *(1 mark)*
   b) 95cm, 90cm, 88cm
      (2 marks for all correct; 1 mark if one incorrect answer)

Module 11: Equations (pages 24–25)

A
1. a 2. c 3. a 4. d 5. a

B
1. a) $a = -13$ b) $b = 7\frac{4}{7}$
2. a) $a = 5$ b) $b = 12$
3. a) $a = 4\frac{4}{5}$ b) $b = -2$
4. a) $a = 11$ b) $b = \frac{2}{7}$
5. a) $a = 1\frac{1}{6}$ b) $b = 2$

C
1. a) $3l = 36 \Rightarrow l = 12$cm *(1 mark)*
   b) $8b = \frac{1}{2} \times 9 \times 4$ *(1 mark)*
      $\Rightarrow b = 18 \div 8 = 2\frac{1}{4}$cm or 2.25cm *(1 mark)*
2. a) $x + 2x + x + 30 + 50 = 360°$ or $4x + 80 = 360°$ *(1 mark)*
   b) 70°, 100°, 140° *(2 marks for all correct, otherwise 1 mark)*

Module 12: Coordinates (pages 26–27)

A
1. b 2. c 3. c 4. d 5. a

B
Accept B and D in either order.

1. a) and b)

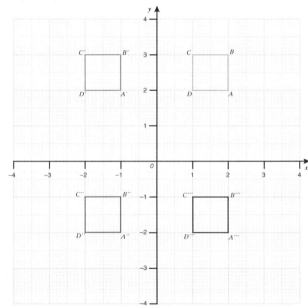

c) $B(2, 3)$, $D(1, 2)$
2. $B'(-1, 3)$, $C'(-2, 3)$, $D'(-2, 2)$
3. a) $B''(-1, -1)$, $C''(-2, -1)$, $D''(-2, -2)$
   b) $B'''(2, -1)$, $C'''(1, -1)$, $D'''(1, -2)$

C
1.

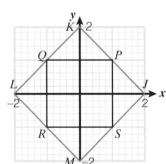

a) and b) *(1 mark)* c) *(1 mark)*
d) $y = -1$ *(1 mark)*
e) No, QS is $y = -x$ which has negative gradient *(1 mark)*

2. a) Any suitable answer, e.g. (6, –2) *(1 mark)*
  b) (6, 6.5) *(1 mark)*, (6, –0.5) *(1 mark)* (Accept 6.4 and –0.4)

Module 13: Functions and graphs (pages 28–29)

A

1. a **2.** c **3.** b **4.** b **5.** d

B

1.

x	–2	–1	0	1	2
y	–12	–7	–2	3	8

2.

x	–2	–1	0	1	2
y	5	–1	–3	–1	5

3.

x	–2	–1	0	1	2
y	11	4	3	2	–5

4.

x	–2	–1	0	1	2
y	0.1	0.3	1	3	9

5.

x	–3	–2	–1	1	2	3
y	–1.7	–2.5	–5	5	2.5	1.7

C

1. a) E. For all the other equations, an x-value of 0, does not produce a y-value of 0. *(1 mark)*
  b) Any of A(0, 3), B(0, –3), C(0, 4), D(0, –4) *(1 mark)*
  c) Any of A(–3, 0), B(3, 0), C(–4, 0), D(4, 0) *(1 mark)*

2. B: $y = 3x – 4$; A: $y = 5x^3$; D: $y = 4 – x$; E: $y = x^2 – 3$; C: $y = \frac{1}{4x}$
  (2 marks for all correct, otherwise 1 mark)

Module 14: Gradients and intercepts (pages 30–31)

A

1. c **2.** a **3.** c **4.** b **5.** a

B

1. a) $m = -\frac{1}{4}, c = \frac{3}{4}$ **b)** $m = 2, c = –8$

2. a)

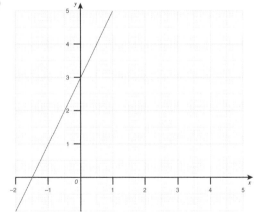

  b)

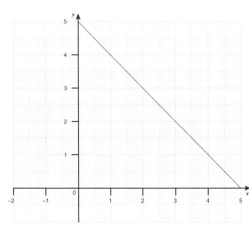

3. a) $m = 2$, 'uphill' **b)** $m = –4$, 'downhill'

4. a) $y = 4 – 3x$ **b)** $2y = x + 5$

C

1. a) Any suitable answer, e.g.

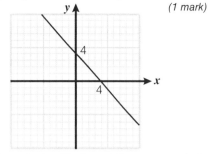

(1 mark)

  b) vertical and horizontal distances equal *(1 mark)*
  c) –1 *(1 mark)*

2.

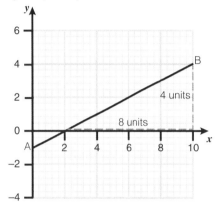

  a) $\frac{4}{8} = \frac{1}{2}$ or 0.5 *(1 mark)*
  b) $y = \frac{1}{2}x – 1$ or $2y = x – 2$ *(1 mark)*
  c) Drawn line *(1 mark)*; gradient = ½ or 0.5 *(1 mark)*
  d) equal *(1 mark)*

3. a) Line drawn through plotted points *(1 mark)*
  b) Gradient = $\frac{10}{5} = 2$. Substitute coordinates into $y = mx + c$ giving y-intercept = –11 *(1 mark)*
  c) $y = 2x – 11$ *(1 mark)*

Module 15: Simultaneous equations (pages 32–33)

A

1. c **2.** b **3.** a **4.** d **5.** a

B

1. $x = 3, y = 4$
2. (0, 1), (2, –1)
3. $x = 1, x = 5$

C

1. 2A + 2C = £24.80, A + 3C = £23.20 *(1 mark)*, child: £5.40, adult: £7.00; *(1 mark)*

2. a) $y = 2x + 3$

x	–1	0	1
y	1	3	5

$2y = 4 – x$

x	–1	0	1
y	2.5	2	1.5

(1 mark for correct tables of coordinates); drawn lines *(1 mark)*;
$a = –0.4$; $b = 2.2$ *(1 mark)*

  b) The solutions of the simultaneous equations *(1 mark)*.

Module 16: Problems and graphs (pages 34–35)

A

1. d **2.** a **3.** b **4.** a **5.** b

B

1.

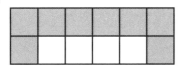

C

1. **a)** May/Jun 2010 *(1 mark)* **b)** Jan/Feb *(1 mark)*, coldest time of year *(1 mark)*

2. **a)** rest for 5 minutes *(1 mark)*

b) $5 \div \frac{1}{4}$ *(1 mark)* = 20mph *(1 mark)*

c) 70 minutes or 1 hour 10 minutes *(1 mark)*

d) $\frac{15}{70} \times 60$ *(1 mark)* = 12.86mph *(1 mark)*

Module 17: Sequences (pages 36–37)

A

1. c **2.** b **3.** b **4.** a **5.** c

B

1. **a)** 64 **b)** 440

2. **a)** $3n$ **b)** $5n + 2$

3. **a)** 27, 38, 51 **b)** 75, 15, 3

4. **a)** (term)^4 **b)** n^4

C

1. $32 - 4n$, 22, 16, 10

(2 marks for all correct, otherwise 1 mark)

2. **a)**

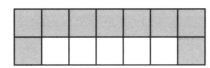

Pattern 4

Pattern 5

(1 mark)

b) $n : (n + 4)$ *(1 mark)*

c) $(10 + 4) = 14$ *(1 mark)*

3. **a)** 63 *(1 mark)*

b) 342 *(1 mark)*

c) 15 624 *(1 mark)*

RATIO, PROPORTION AND RATES OF CHANGE

Module 18: Converting measurements (pages 38–39)

A

1. c **2.** c **3.** a **4.** b **5.** b

B

1. **a)** 82.5km/h **b)** 62.5mph

2. **a)** 11.05am, 1.12pm **b)** 2 hours 7 minutes

3. **a)** 250cl **b)** 4.4 pints

C

1. **a)** Dec 2 *(1 mark)* **b)** Dec 3 *(1 mark)*

c) Dec 3, 12 hours 26 minutes *(1 mark)*

2. **a)** 300ml *(1 mark)* **b)** 125g *(1 mark)* **c)** 4m *(1 mark)*

Module 19: Scales, diagrams and maps (pages 40–41)

A

1. d **2.** c **3.** a **4.** b **5.** d

B

1. **a)** 80cm **b)** 54cm

2. **a)** 84km **b)** 062°

3. **a)** Line of 4.8cm drawn **b)** Line of 13mm drawn

C

1. **a)**

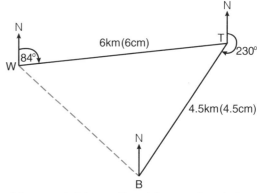

(1 mark for correct distances, 1 mark for correct angles)

b) 3.5km, 135° *(1 mark)*

2. **a)** $13 \times 20 = 260$m *(1 mark)* **b)** $210 \div 20 = 10.5$cm *(1 mark)*

Module 20: Comparing quantities (pages 42–43)

A

1. c **2.** a **3.** d **4.** a **5.** c

B

1. **a)** $\frac{31}{52}$ **b)** $\frac{7}{10}$

2. **a)** 18% **b)** 21%

3. **a)** $\frac{23}{26}$ **b)** 11.5%

C

1. **a)** $\frac{5}{12} \times \frac{3}{5} = \frac{1}{4}$ *(1 mark)*

b) $\frac{2}{5} \times 80 = 32$ *(1 mark)*

c) $\frac{36}{80} = \frac{9}{20}$ or $\frac{1}{4} + \frac{1}{5} = \frac{9}{20}$ *(1 mark)*

2. Smarts: $1.20 \times 599.99 = £719.99$ *(1 mark)* > Wises: £699.99 Wises is the better buy *(1 mark)*.

Module 21: Ratio (pages 44–45)

A

1. a **2.** c **3.** d **4.** b **5.** b

B

1. **a)** $2 : 9 : 7$ **b)** $3 : 5 : 8$

2. **a)** £92, £230, £138 **b)** 150ml : 375ml : 225ml

3. **a)** $3 : 2 : 1$ **b)** £4.50, £3, £1.50

4. **a)** $\frac{2}{5}$

b) strawberries : blueberries : raspberries = 6 : 10 : 9

C

1. **a)** $(5 \times 7.5) \div 6 = 6.3$cm, *(1 mark)* $(7 \times 7.5) \div 6 = 8.8$cm *(1 mark)*

b) $(5 \times 12) \div 7 = 8.6$cm, *(1 mark)* $(6 \times 12) \div 7 = 10.3$cm *(1 mark)*

2. **a)** $10 \times 6 \div 5 = 12$; $12 \times 3 \div 2 = 18$ *(1 mark)*

b) $10 : 12 : 18 = 5 : 6 : 9$ *(1 mark)*

c) £80 ÷ 20 = £4 ⇒ £20, £24, £36 *(1 mark)*

Module 22: Percentage change (pages 46–47)

A

1. b **2.** d **3.** a **4.** d **5.** c

B

1. **a)** 600g **b)** 900g

2. **a)** £74.80 **b)** £90.64

3. **a)** £367.50 **b)** £688.01

C

1. **a)** $0.95 \times 3.4 = 3.23$kg *(1 mark)*

b) 3.37kg − 3.23kg = 0.14kg ⇒ 20g/day *(1 mark)*

c) $\frac{3.6}{3.4} \times 100$ *(1 mark)* = 106% *(1 mark)*

2.

Occupation	2011	% change	2012
pharmacists	£36 045	+3.7	£37 379
paramedics	£36 500	+1.7	£37 120
vets	£37 413	−9.9	£33 709
midwives	£28 930	+1.1	£29 248
physiotherapists	£26 000	+2.4	£26 625

(2 marks if fully correct; 1 mark for up to two incorrect answers)

Module 23: Proportion (pages 48–49)

A

1. d   **2.** c   **3.** a   **4.** b   **5.** b

B

1. a) £196   **b)** £280

2. a) £5.96   **b)** £8.34

3. a) 21 mins   **b)** 72*l*

4. a) $3\frac{1}{3}$ days   **b)** £570

C

1. 5000 ÷ 3.75 = 1333.$\dot{3}$ *(1 mark)*

2. a) 30 ÷ 5 = 6 *(1 mark)*

     b) 6 × £18 = £108 *(1 mark)*

     c) $\frac{8}{20} = \frac{2}{5}$ *(1 mark)*

     d) £72 ÷ 12 = 6 *(1 mark)* ⇒ 6 × 8 = 48 wraps *(1 mark)*

GEOMETRY AND MEASURES

Module 24: Perimeter, area and volume (pages 50–51)

A

1. a   **2.** d   **3.** b   **4.** b   **5.** c

B

1. a) 28.14m²   **b)** £252.98   **c)** 21.04m

2. a) 23.37cm²   **b)** 51.3cm²

3. a) 31.4cm   **b)** 59.22cm²

4. a) 14.1cm, 9.45cm   **b)** 47.2cm

C

1. a) 8 × 30cm = 240cm *(1 mark)*, 240cm × 240cm or
       2.4m × 2.4m *(1 mark)*

     b) 57 600cm² or 5.76m² *(1 mark)*

     c) Cost = (24 × £5.93) + (20 × £9.36) *(1 mark)*
        = £142.32 + £187.20 = £329.52 *(1 mark)*

2. Sum of equal sides > 3rd side *(1 mark)*
     ∴ 4 possible triangles: 5, 5, 7; 6, 6, 5; 7, 7, 3; 8, 8, 1 *(1 mark)*

Module 25: Circles (pages 52–53)

A

1. c   **2.** a   **3.** d   **4.** a   **5.** d

B

1. a) 4.27cm   **b)** 57.16cm²

2. a) 154cm²   **b)** 42cm²

3. a) 282.74cm²   **b)** 371.10cm²

     c) 530.14cm³ or 0.53 litres

C

1. a) $C = \pi \times 2.3 = 7.23$cm *(1 mark)*

     b) 10 000 ÷ 7.23 *(1 mark)* = 1383 (nearest whole number) *(1 mark)*

2. a) $d = \sqrt{(6^2 + 6^2)}$ *(1 mark)* $= \sqrt{72} = 8.49$cm (2 d.p.) *(1 mark)*

     b) $r = \frac{d}{2} = 4.245$cm, $A = \pi(4.245)^2 = 56.6$cm² (3 s.f.) *(1 mark)*

Module 26: Constructions (pages 54–55)

A

1. b   **2.** a   **3.** b   **4.** d   **5.** c

B

1. a) 5cm

     b)

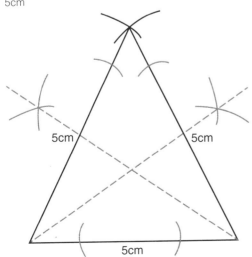

2. a) to **d)**

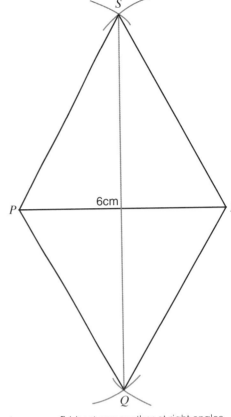

     e) rhombus   **f)** bisect one another at right angles

3. a) 45°   **b)** Accept 7.3–7.4cm   **c)** 105°

C

1.

(2 marks for all measurements correct, otherwise 1 mark)

2. a) pentagon *(1 mark)*

     b) Correct drawing *(1 mark)*; $BQ = QC = 3.5$cm *(1 mark)*

     c) They are equal. PE is perpendicular bisector of BC *(1 mark)*

Module 27: Properties of 2D shapes (pages 56–57)

A

1. d   **2.** c   **3.** a   **4.** a   **5.** b

B

1. a) regular octagon   **b)** parallelogram, rhombus

2. a) isosceles   **b) i)** rhombus   **ii)** 16cm²

3. a) isosceles trapezium

     b) i) isosceles triangle   **ii)** pentagon

C

1. a) Yes, both have six sides *(1 mark)*

     b) No, the sides of the second shape are not equal *(1 mark)*

2.

Polygon	Side	Perimeter	Exterior angle	Interior angle
pentagon	6.5cm	32.5cm	72°	108°
octagon	6.5cm	52cm	45°	135°
decagon	5cm	50cm	36°	144°

(2 marks for all correct; 1 mark if one row is incorrect)

3. Correct drawing *(1 mark)*; trapezium *(1 mark)*

Module 28: Transformations (pages 58–59)
A
1. c **2.** b **3.** a **4.** a **5.** d
B

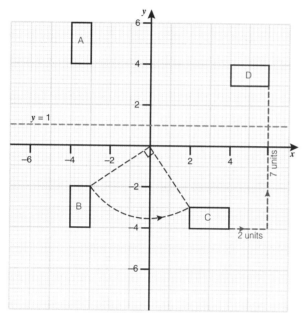

1. reflection in line $y = 1$ or translation $\begin{pmatrix} 0 \\ -8 \end{pmatrix}$ or rotation of 180° about $(-3.5, 1)$
2. rotation of 90° anticlockwise about (0, 0) or rotation of 270° clockwise about (0, 0)
3. translation $\begin{pmatrix} 2 \\ 7 \end{pmatrix}$
4. rotation of 90° anticlockwise about the origin (0, 0) or rotation of 270° clockwise about (0, 0)
C
1. a) C *(1 mark)* **b)** hexagon *(1 mark)*, kite *(1 mark)*
2. a) 5 *(1 mark)* **b)** 6 *(1 mark)* **c)** 3 *(1 mark)*

Module 29: Congruence and similarity (pages 60–61)
A
1. b **2.** d **3.** a **4.** c **5.** a
B
1. a) similar **b)** 2 : 3
c) 2.67cm **d)** 2.5cm
2. a) 51.6cm **b)** 8.6cm
C
1. scale factor = $\frac{12}{17}$ *(1 mark)* $\therefore \frac{PS}{PS+13} = \frac{12}{17} \Rightarrow 17PS = 12(PS + 13)$ *(1 mark)*
$\Rightarrow 5PS = 156$
$\Rightarrow PS = 31.2$m *(1 mark)*

2.

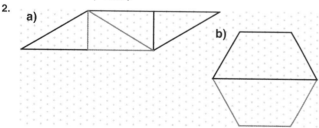

a) i) and **ii)** See diagram above *(1 mark)*
iii) See diagram above *(1 mark)*
b) See diagram above *(1 mark)*

Module 30: Angle facts (pages 62–63)
A
1. b **2.** a **3.** d **4.** a **5.** b
B
1. a) 32°, 148°, 148° **b)** 110°, 70°, 70°
2. a) 61°, 119°, 119° **b)** 61°, 61°, 119°, 119°
3. a) 51.4° **b)** 900°
C
1. a) Exterior angle = 45° Sum of interior angles = 1080° *(1 mark)*
b) Exterior angle = 36° Sum of interior angles = 1440° *(1 mark)*
2. a) Obtuse angle = 3 (sum of acute angles)
$\Rightarrow$ obtuse angle = $3 \times \frac{180°}{4} = 3 \times 45° = 135°$ *(1 mark)*
b) 15°, 30° *(1 mark)*
3. $a = 127°$ (angles at a point); $b = 138°$ (angles on a straight line);
$c = 46°$ (angle sum of triangle); $d = 49°$ (90° – 41°)
(2 marks if all correct; 1 mark if one incorrect answer)

Module 31: Pythagoras' theorem and trigonometry (pages 64–65)
A
1. c **2.** d **3.** b **4.** b **5.** c
B
1. a) 26mm **b)** 30.9cm
2. a) 2.5cm **b)** 3.12cm
3. a) no **b)** yes
4. a) 36.2cm **b)** 48.6°
c) 9.4cm **d)** 38.4°
C
1. Use Pythagoras' theorem:
LHS = $16.5^2 = 272.25$cm²; RHS = $8.9^2 + 10.8^2 = 79.21 + 116.69$
= 195.85cm² ≠ LHS *(1 mark)*
Triangle is not right-angled *(1 mark)*
2. 14.4cm *(1 mark)*
3. a) $A = \frac{1}{2} \times 6 \times 12 = 36$cm² *(1 mark)*
b) $PS = \sqrt{(9^2 + 12^2)} = 15$cm *(1 mark)*
c) $\tan PQR = \frac{12}{15} \Rightarrow \angle PQR = 38.7°$ *(1 mark)*

Module 32: Properties of 3D shapes (pages 66–67)
A
1. d **2.** a **3.** c **4.** b **5.** c
B
1. a) 78.5cm² **b)** 636 **c)** 65.4cm³
2. a) 17.43cm³ **b)** 48.38cm²
3. a) 20cm **b)** 9048cm³ **c)** 2139cm²
C
1. No. of cubes = 3 × 4 × 10 *(1 mark)* = 120 *(1 mark)*
2. a) $\frac{1}{2} \times 6 \times 4 \times 12$ *(1 mark)* = 144cm³ *(1 mark)*
b) $l = \sqrt{(3^2 + 4^2)} = 5$cm *(1 mark)*
$A = (2 \times \frac{1}{2} \times 6 \times 4) + (6 \times 12) + 2(5 \times 12)$
= 24 + 72 + 120 = 216cm² *(1 mark)*
3. Inner cylinder diameter = 6cm, height = 18cm *(1 mark)*
Capacity = π(3)² × 18 = 508.9cm³ *(1 mark)*

PROBABILITY

Module 33: Experimental probability (pages 68–69)
A
1. b **2.** a **3.** d **4.** c **5.** c
B
1. a) $\frac{1}{2}$ **b)** $\frac{1}{6}$ **c)** $\frac{1}{3}$
2. a) $\frac{1}{5}$ **b)** $\frac{2}{5}$ **c)** 0
3. a) $\frac{1}{3}$ **b)** $\frac{13}{18}$
4. a) $\frac{3}{8}$ **b)** $\frac{7}{8}$
C
1. a) P(A, E, I or O) = $\frac{45}{120}$ *(1 mark)* = $\frac{3}{8}$ *(1 mark)*
b) P(not I, not O) = $\frac{100}{120}$ *(1 mark)* = $\frac{5}{6}$ *(1 mark)*
c) P(P, Q or S) = $\frac{3}{20} \Rightarrow \frac{18}{120}$ (mult. 6) *(1 mark)*
Sum of ratio parts = 9; 18 ÷ 9 = 2 (1 part) *(1 mark)*
$\therefore$ P(2 × 2) = 4; Q(3 × 2) = 6; R(4 × 2) = 8 *(1 mark)*

2. Lose, $\frac{5}{12} < \frac{1}{2}$ *(1 mark)*
3. 2, 4, 6, 8, 10

   (2 marks if all correct, otherwise 1 mark)

Module 34: Theoretical probability (pages 70–71)

A

1. b **2.** a **3.** a **4.** c **5.** a

B

1. **a)** $\frac{12}{25}$ **b)** $\frac{24}{125}$ **c)** $\frac{13}{25}$
2. **a)** $\frac{1}{8}$ **b)** $\frac{3}{8}$
3. **a)** $\frac{4}{9}$ **b)** $\frac{5}{18}$

C

1. P(even total) = $\frac{8}{16} = \frac{1}{2}$ *(1 mark)*

	2	4	6	8
1	3	5	7	9
2	4	6	8	10
3	5	7	9	11
4	6	8	10	12

(1 mark)

2. **a)**

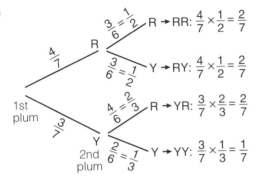

   (2 marks if tree fully correct; 1 mark if one or two errors in tree)
   b) P(RR) or P(YY) = $\frac{2}{7} + \frac{1}{7} = \frac{3}{7}$ *(1 mark)*
   c) P(not choosing Y) = $\frac{4}{7} \times \frac{1}{2} = \frac{2}{7}$ *(1 mark)*
3. $(0.2 \times 0.7) + (0.8 \times 0.3)$ *(1 mark)* = 0.14 + 0.24 = 0.38 *(1 mark)*

Module 35: Sets (pages 72–73)

A

1. d **2.** a **3.** d **4.** a **5.** b

B

1. **a)** 7 **b)** 5 **c)** 2 **d)** 25
2. **a)** {1, 4, 8, 9, 16, 25, 27, 36, 49, 64, 81, 100, 121, 125, 144}
   b) {1, 64}
   c) {4, 8, 16, 36, 64, 100, 144}
3. **a)** {1, 2, 4} **b)** 4

C

1. **a)** 1, 2, 4, 8, 16, 32, 64 *(1 mark)*
   b) 9, 18, 27, 36, 45, 54, 63, 72, 81, 90, 99 *(1 mark)*
   c) 19, 29, 59, 79, 89 *(1 mark)*
2. **a)** 39 *(1 mark)* **b)** 13 *(1 mark)* **c)** 60 *(1 mark)*
   d) Any suitable answer, e.g. listen to audiobooks,
   don't read *(1 mark)*

STATISTICS

Module 36: Data (pages 74–75)

A

1. c **2.** d **3.** c **4.** b **5.** d

B

1. Any suitable answers:
   a) Which age range are you?

   <16yrs ☐ 17–24yrs ☐ 25–39yrs ☐ 40yrs+ ☐

   b) When do you watch TV?

   never ☐ morning ☐ afternoon ☐ evening ☐

   c) Rate 'The Main Chance' from 1 to 10 (10 is top).

2. **a)**

Cheese	Red Leicester	Cheddar	Cheshire	Lancashire	Wensleydale
Frequency	17	35	30	28	15

   b) 125 **c)** cheddar

C

1. There are 38 right-handed boys; There are 14 left-handed students;
   There are 96 students in the year.
   (2 marks for all correct, otherwise 1 mark)
2. **a)** Any suitable answer, e.g. just people going into newsagents,
   not cross-section of community, depends on time of
   recording *(1 mark)*
   b) Any suitable answer, e.g. middle of high street, place with
   better selection of shops *(1 mark)*
   c) Any suitable answer, e.g. store owners for planning, local
   transport planning *(1 mark)*

Module 37: Averages (pages 76–77)

A

1. c **2.** b **3.** a **4.** d **5.** b

B

1. **a)** 120 **b)** 2 **c)** 1.725 **d)** 2
2. **a)** 65 **b)** 66 **c)** 66 **d)** mean using all marks

C

1. Total number of raisins = $(39 \times 2) + (40 \times 0) + (41 \times 3) + (42 \times 2) +$
   $(43 \times 3) + (44 \times 1) = 78 + 0 + 123 + 84 + 129 + 44 = 458$ *(1 mark)*,
   total given = $12 \times 42 = 504$
   ∴ no. of raisins in 12th bag = $504 - 458 = 46$ *(1 mark)*
2. **a)** 5 *(1 mark)*
   b) **i)** median = 5, mode = 5 *(1 mark)*
   ii) $[(2 \times 1) + (3 \times 2) + (4 \times 10) + (5 \times 21) + (6 \times 16) +$
   $(7 \times 2)] \div 52$ *(1 mark)*
   $= 263 \div 52 = 5.06$ *(1 mark)*
   iii) Mode: gives the size of most students *(1 mark)*

Module 38: Charts and diagrams (pages 78–79)

A

1. c **2.** d **3.** c **4.** b **5.** b

B

1.

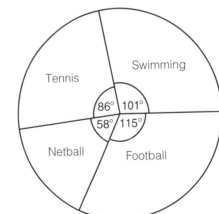

2. **a)** negative **b)** Accept 25–30

C

1. **a)** 1700 million *(1 mark)* **b)** 2011 *(1 mark)*
   c) 8000 million *(1 mark)*
2. **a)** 99cm *(1 mark)* **b)** 10/30 *(1 mark)* = $33\frac{1}{3}\%$ *(1 mark)*

MIXED TEST-STYLE QUESTIONS

1. **a)** 32 days *(1 mark)* **b)** $\frac{16}{183}$ *(1 mark)*

2. Burgers: 15, Steaks: 2.5kg, Sausages: 1.75kg, Barbecue sauce: 750ml, Baked potatoes: 15, Coleslaw: 1875g, Baked beans: 400g
    (3 marks if fully correct; 2 marks if one or two answers incorrect; 1 mark if at least three answers correct)

3. **a)** $y = -3x + 5$ *(1 mark)*
    b) gradient = -3, y-intercept is $(0, 5)$ *(1 mark)*
    c) parallel line has gradient = -3 *(1 mark)*. Substitute -3 and $(2, 3)$ into $y = mx + c$ giving $c = 9$, equation is $y = -3x + 9$ *(1 mark)*

4. L takes $\frac{150}{60} = 2\frac{1}{2}$ hours *(1 mark)*; M's speed = $\frac{80}{2.5}$ = 32km/h *(2 marks)*

5. **a)** $y, y - 13, y - 6$
    (2 marks if fully correct; 1 mark if one error)
    b) $y + y - 13 + y - 6 = 50$ *(1 mark)* $\Rightarrow 3y - 19 = 50 \Rightarrow 3y = 69$ *(1 mark)* $\Rightarrow y = 23$ and sides = 23cm, 10cm, 17cm *(1 mark)*

6. **a)**

Cuboid	Dimensions		
A	20	1	1
B	10	1	2
C	5	4	1
D	5	2	2

(2 marks if fully correct; 1 mark if two rows correct)

   b) A (82 square units) *(1 mark)*, as B is 64 square units, C is 58 square units and D is 48 square units *(1 mark)*
   c) A, B, C and D are each 20 cubed units *(1 mark)*, so the volume of each cuboid is equal *(1 mark)*.

7. **a)** 28 *(1 mark)*
    b) 110cm *(1 mark)*
    c) 111.5cm *(2 marks)*
    d) $122 - 100 = 22$cm *(1 mark)*

8. **a)** P(good plum) = $\frac{56}{60} = \frac{14}{15}$ *(1 mark)*
    b) P(good pear and a mouldy plum) = $\frac{38}{40} \times \frac{4}{60}$ *(1 mark)* = $\frac{38}{600} = \frac{19}{300}$ *(1 mark)*
    c) Ratio of pears to plums in display = 38 : 56 = 19 : 28 *(1 mark)*

9. Area = $15a^2 = 5a \times 3a$; Perimeter = $2(5a + 3a) = 16a$
    Length = $5a$cm *(1 mark)*; Width = $3a$cm *(1 mark)*

10. **a)** Positive correlation *(1 mark)*
    b) Accept any answer between 32–34mm *(1 mark)*
    c) No, this measurement is too far from line of best fit *(1 mark)*

11. **a)** $A \cup B = \{3, 5, 6, 9\}$ *(1 mark)*
    b) $A \cap B = \{15, 30, 45, 60\}$ *(1 mark)*

12. 8: line symmetry, rotational symmetry
    P: no symmetry
    Z: rotational symmetry
    6: no symmetry
    Y: line symmetry
    (2 marks if fully correct; 1 mark for at least three correct)

13. **a)** 50 000 000 *(1 mark)*; 5×10^7 *(1 mark)*
    b) $409 000 000 *(1 mark)*
    c) $0.15 \times \$408 992 272 = \$61 348 840.80$ *(1 mark)* = $61 348 800 (nearest $100) *(1 mark)*

14. **a)** 2.935 405 617 *(1 mark)*
    b) $(92 \times \sqrt{4}) \div (65 - 10) = \frac{162}{55} \approx 3$ *(1 mark)*

15. **a)** $\frac{5}{9}(35.6 - 32) = \frac{18}{9} = 2°C$ *(1 mark)*
    b) $(23 \times \frac{9}{5}) + 32 = 41.4 + 32 = 73.4°F$ *(1 mark)*

16. **a)** $\frac{1}{3} \times 2\pi \times 12.5 = 26.2$cm *(1 mark)*
    b) $\frac{3}{4} \times 2\pi \times 12.5 = 58.9$cm *(1 mark)*
    c) $24 \times 2\pi \times 12.5$ *(1 mark)* = 1885.0cm *(1 mark)*

17. **a)** $a = 14.6 \times \frac{10.5}{21} = 7.3$cm *(1 mark)*
    $b = 11 \times \frac{21}{10.5} = 22$cm *(1 mark)*
    b) AE is parallel to BC as $\angle A$ and $\angle C$ are alternate angles *(1 mark)*

18. **a)** $53 \times 41 \times 31 = 67 363$cm³ *(1 mark)*
    b) $53 \times 37 \times 31 = 60 791$cm³ *(1 mark)*
    c) £120 − £(99 + 6.20 + 4.20 + 2.49) *(1 mark)* = £120 − £111.89 = £8.11 *(1 mark)*

19.

Scale	Design dimension	Actual dimension
1 : 10	6.4cm	64cm
1 : 8	17cm	1.36m
1 : 20	20cm	4m
1 : 2.5	9cm	22.5cm
1 : 250	4.8cm	12m
1 : 75	11cm	825cm

(1 mark for each correctly completed column)

20. **a)** $0.642 - 0.6 = 0.042$m = 42mm *(1 mark)*
    b) $3721 \div 6 = 620.17$mm
    (1 mark for 3721 and 1 mark for correct answer)

Answer all parts of the questions. Use a separate sheet of paper if necessary.

1 A set of three circular biscuit cutters sit inside one another.

Their diameters are in the ratio 5 : 6 : 7 ⊞

a) The diameter of the middle cutter is 7.5cm. What are the diameters of the other two cutters?

Show all your working, giving the diameters to 1 decimal place.

.... cm and .... cm   (2 marks)

b) There is another set of cutters for larger biscuits. Their diameters are in the same ratio.

The diameter of the largest cutter is 12cm. What are the diameters of the other two cutters?

Show all your working, giving the diameters to 1 decimal place.

.... cm and .... cm   (2 marks)

2 Three children are given birthday money, totalling £80, in the same ratio as their ages.

The youngest child is 10 years old. This is $\frac{5}{6}$ of the age of the middle child.

The middle child's age is $\frac{2}{3}$ of the age of the eldest child.

a) What are the ages of the middle and eldest children?

Show all your working.

(1 mark)

b) What is the ratio of the ages of the three children?

Show all your working.

(1 mark)

c) How much money do they each receive?

Show all your working.

(1 mark)

Score   /7

For more help on this topic see KS3 Maths Revision Guide pages 48–49.

A — Choose just one answer, a, b, c or d.

1 £90 increased by 5% is: (1 mark)
   a) £104.50 ☐   **b)** £94.50 ☐
   c) £91.50 ☐   **d)** £99 ☐

2 £140 decreased by 12% is: (1 mark)
   a) £128 ☐   **b)** £126.50 ☐
   c) £124 ☐   **d)** £123.20 ☐

3 What multiplier should be used for an increase of 11%? (1 mark)
   a) 1.11 ☐   **b)** 1.21 ☐
   c) 1.01 ☐   **d)** 1.09 ☐

4 The original value of a dishwasher, costing £380 after a 10% discount, is: (1 mark)
   a) £395.50 ☐   **b)** £390 ☐
   c) £400 ☐   **d)** £422.22 ☐

5 How much annual interest at 3.3% would be paid on £1250? (1 mark)
   a) £40 ☐   **b)** £42.50 ☐
   c) £41.25 ☐   **d)** £43.33 ☐

Score /5

B — Answer all parts of each question.

1 A box of cereal includes 20% extra free. How much cereal is now in these two sizes? Give your answers in grams.

   a) 500g

   .... (1 mark)

   b) 750g

   .... (1 mark)

2 A hotel normally charges £88 per person per night per room if two people share.

   a) What is the room rate if there is a special offer of 15% discount?

   .... (1 mark)

   b) A single person has to pay a supplement of 3% extra. How much do they pay?

   .... (1 mark)

3 A bank advertises a special account paying 3.5% per annum on savings for six months, then 3% per annum over the next six months.

   a) How much will be earned on £21 000 after six months?

   .... (1 mark)

   b) How much will be earned on the total savings in the account by the end of a year?

   .... (1 mark)

Score /6

Answer all parts of the questions. Use a separate sheet of paper if necessary.

1 A newborn baby weighs 3.4kg.

When the baby is a week old, his weight has decreased by 5%. 🔲

a) What is the baby's weight after one week?

Show all your working.

.... kg   (1 mark)

b) When the baby is two weeks old, his weight is 3.37kg.

He gains weight by an equal amount each day of the second week.

How much is his daily weight gain?

Show all your working.

.... g/day   (1 mark)

c) At six months, he weighs 7kg.

What is his percentage weight gain over his birth weight?

Show all your working.

(2 marks)

2 This table shows the average annual salary for 2012 with the percentage change from 2011.

Occupation	2011 salary	% change	2012 salary
pharmacists	£36045	+3.7	£
paramedics	£36500		£37120
vets	£37413	−9.9	£
midwives	£	+1.1	£29248
physiotherapists	£26000		£26625

Complete the table.

Show all your working. 🔲

(2 marks)

Score   /6

For more help on this topic see KS3 Maths Revision Guide pages 50–51.

A Choose just one answer, a, b, c or d.

1 A car travels 300m in 20 seconds. How far will it travel in one minute? *(1 mark)*

a) 600m ☐   **b)** 150m ☐

c) 320m ☐   **d)** 900m ☐

2 A recipe needs 115g raisins for five people. How much is needed for 12 people? *(1 mark)*

a) 274g ☐   **b)** 275g ☐

c) 276g ☐   **d)** 300g ☐

3 A room can be decorated in four days by one man. How long will two men take? *(1 mark)*

a) 2 days ☐   **b)** 1.5 days ☐

c) 3 days ☐   **d)** 3.5 days ☐

4 £1 will buy $1.61
How much will £120 buy? *(1 mark)*

a) $123.20 ☐

b) $193.20 ☐

c) $161.10 ☐

d) $100 ☐

5 One litre of petrol costs £1.28
How much will it cost to fill a 45*l* tank? *(1 mark)*

a) £56.70 ☐

b) £57.60 ☐

c) £47.60 ☐

d) £65.60 ☐

Score   /5

B Answer all parts of each question.

1 Six friends are going to a concert. Their tickets cost a total of £168. Another friend decides to join them.

a) What is the total bill for the tickets? .... *(1 mark)*

b) What would be the bill for 10 tickets? .... *(1 mark)*

2 A 2.5kg bag of potatoes costs £2.98. What is the cost of: *(2 marks)*

a) 5kg? ....   **b)** 7kg? ....

3 A paddling pool holds 50 litres of water. It is filled at a rate of 12 litres of water every five minutes.

a) How long, to the nearest minute, will it take to fill the pool?

.... *(1 mark)*

b) What size pool could be filled in 30 minutes?

.... *(1 mark)*

4 Two gardeners, working six hours each day, can landscape a garden in five days.

a) How many working days would three gardeners take?

.... *(1 mark)*

b) The gardeners each charge £9.50 per hour. How much do the gardeners cost?

.... *(1 mark)*

Score   /8

Answer all parts of the questions. Use a separate sheet of paper if necessary.

1 The unreleased energy contained in the average dustbin each year could power a TV for 5000 hours.

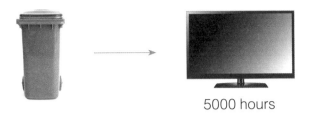

5000 hours

The average evening TV viewing is 3 hours 45 minutes.

How many evenings of TV viewing could be powered by the average dustbin in a year?

Show all your working. 🖩

.... evenings   (1 mark)

2 A supermarket packs platters of 24 assorted sandwiches, which cost £18 per platter.

This serves about five people.

A customer is having a tea party for 30 people.

a) How many platters should she order for the tea party?

Show all your working.

(1 mark)

b) How much will the platters cost?

Show all your working.

(1 mark)

Another platter, costing £12, contains 12 sandwiches and 8 wraps.

c) What proportion of the platter is wraps?

Show all your working.

(1 mark)

d) A number of these platters cost £72 in total.

How many wraps were on these platters?

Show all your working.

(2 marks)

Score   /6

For more help on this topic see KS3 Maths Revision Guide pages 52–53.

A Choose just one answer, a, b, c or d.

1 The perimeter of a square
of side 3.5cm is: (1 mark)
a) 14cm ☐ b) 12.25cm ☐
c) 7cm ☐ d) 10.5cm ☐

2 The area of the square in
question 1 is: (1 mark)
a) 14cm² ☐ b) 7cm² ☐
c) 10.50cm² ☐ d) 12.25cm² ☐

3 If the square in question 1 is the face
of a cube, what is the cube's volume
to 3 s.f.? (1 mark)
a) 32.5cm³ ☐ b) 42.9cm³ ☐
c) 42.5cm³ ☐ d) 32.9cm³ ☐

4 The surface area of the cube in
question 3 is: (1 mark)
a) 62.5cm² ☐
b) 73.5cm² ☐
c) 72.25cm² ☐
d) 62.25cm² ☐

5 Two of the cubes in question 3 are
stuck together to make a cuboid.
Its surface area is: (1 mark)
a) 225cm² ☐
b) 122cm² ☐
c) 122.5cm² ☐
d) 1225cm² ☐

Score /5

B Answer all parts of each question.

1 A carpet is to be fitted in a room 6.7m × 4.2m.

a) What area of carpet is needed?

.... (1 mark)

b) A square metre of the carpet costs £8.99. How much does it cost to carpet
the room?

.... (1 mark)

c) The room has a door 76cm wide. What length of skirting board is in the room?

.... (1 mark)

2 A triangle and a parallelogram both have a perpendicular height of 5.7cm. What is
the area of:

a) the triangle with a base of 8.2cm? .... (1 mark)

b) the parallelogram with a base of 9cm? .... (1 mark)

3 A rectangle has a length of 9.4cm and a width of 6.3cm. Work out its:

a) perimeter .... (1 mark)

b) area .... (1 mark)

4 A parallelogram has sides 1.5 times the rectangle in question 3. Work out:

a) the length of its sides .... (1 mark)

b) its perimeter .... (1 mark)

Score /9

1   A conservatory floor has grey and white tiles:

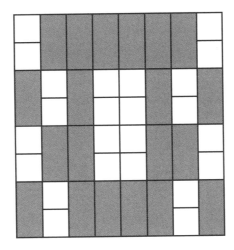

The side of one square white tile measures 30cm.

a) What are the dimensions of the conservatory floor?

Show all your working.

(2 marks)

b) What is the area of the conservatory floor?

Show all your working.

(1 mark)

c) A white tile costs £5.93. A grey tile costs £9.36.

Work out the cost of tiling the conservatory floor.

Show all your working.

(2 marks)

2   A triangle is described as having a perimeter of 17cm and two equal sides. Each side measures a whole number of centimetres.

Work out how many possible versions of this triangle there are.

There is no need to construct the triangles.

(2 marks)

Score   /7

For more help on this topic see KS3 Maths Revision Guide pages 56–57.

A   **Choose just one answer, a, b, c or d.**

1 The radius of a circle with
diameter 5.8cm is: (1 mark)
   a) 2.4cm ☐   **b)** 2.5cm ☐
   c) 2.9cm ☐   **d)** 2.8cm ☐

2 The circumference of the circle in
question 1 in terms of π is: (1 mark)
   a) 5.8πcm ☐   **b)** 6πcm ☐
   c) 2.9πcm ☐   **d)** 5πcm ☐

3 The area of the circle in question 1 in
terms of π is: (1 mark)
   a) 10.4πcm^2 ☐   **b)** 9.4πcm^2 ☐
   c) 9πcm^2 ☐   **d)** 8.41πcm^2 ☐

4 The circle in question 1 is the cross-
section of a cylinder (of height 7cm).
What is the volume of the
cylinder?   (1 mark)
   a) 58.9πcm^3 ☐
   b) 58.8πcm^3 ☐
   c) 58.7πcm^3 ☐
   d) 58.6πcm^3 ☐

5 The circle in question 1 is cut in half.
What is the semicircle's perimeter to
the nearest whole number?   (1 mark)
   a) 22cm ☐   **b)** 10cm ☐
   c) 12cm ☐   **d)** 15cm ☐

Score   **/5**

B   **Answer all parts of each question. Use the π key on your calculator.**

1 A circle has a circumference of 26.8cm. Giving answers to 2 d.p., work out its:

   a) radius .... (1 mark)

   b) area .... (1 mark)

2 A photo-frame is made from a square of side 14cm with a circle, touching each
side, cut out from its centre. Work out the following areas in cm^2.

←— 14cm —→

   a) the cut-out .... (1 mark)

   b) the shaded part .... (1 mark)

3 A cylindrical can of baked beans of height 12cm and diameter 7.5cm has a label
covering its curved side.

Work out (to 2 d.p.):

   a) the area of the label .... (1 mark)

   b) the surface area of tin needed to make the can .... (1 mark)

   c) the capacity of the can .... (1 mark)

Score   **/7**

1 This cotton reel has a diameter of 2.3cm.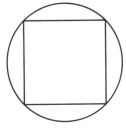

a) Work out the cotton reel's circumference to 2 decimal places.

Show all your working.

.... cm   (1 mark)

b) The label states that it has 100m of cotton around it.

How many times does the cotton go around the reel?

Show all your working. Give your answer to the nearest whole number.

(2 marks)

2 This diagram shows a square with each vertex touching the circumference of a circle.

The square has a side of 6cm.

a) Work out the diameter of the circle to 2 decimal places.

Show all your working.

.... cm   (2 marks)

b) Use your answer in part **a)** to work out the area of the circle to 3 significant figures.

Show all your working.

.... cm²   (1 mark)

Score **/6**

For more help on this topic see KS3 Maths Revision Guide pages 58–59.

A **Choose just one answer, a, b, c or d.**

1 Bisect means to cut into: (1 mark)
   a) four quarters ☐
   b) two halves ☐
   c) three thirds ☐
   d) five fifths ☐

2 Perpendicular means at an angle of: (1 mark)
   a) 90° ☐ **b)** 45° ☐
   c) 60° ☐ **d)** 180° ☐

3 Part of a circumference is: (1 mark)
   a) a section ☐ **b)** an arc ☐
   c) a sector ☐ **d)** a chord ☐

4 A protractor is used to measure: (1 mark)
   a) a line ☐
   b) the radius ☐
   c) the circumference ☐
   d) an angle ☐

5 A perpendicular bisector: (1 mark)
   a) cuts a right angle into two exact halves ☐
   b) cuts a right angle into three exact thirds ☐
   c) cuts a line into two exact halves at right angles ☐
   d) cuts a line at 60° into two exact halves ☐

Score /5

B **Answer each question, using a separate sheet of paper as necessary.**

1 A flower bed is in the shape of an equilateral triangle of side 1.5m.

   The centre of the flower bed is marked by a post. A diagram of the flower bed is drawn to a scale of 1 : 30.

   a) What will each side of the flower bed measure on the diagram?

   .... (1 mark)

   b) Use a ruler and a pair of compasses to construct a diagram of the flower bed to the given scale. (1 mark)

2 **a)** Draw a line PR = 6cm (1 mark)

   b) Construct the perpendicular bisector of PR. (1 mark)

   c) Label the arc intersections Q and S. (1 mark)

   d) Join $P \rightarrow Q \rightarrow R \rightarrow S \rightarrow P$ and $Q \rightarrow S$. (1 mark)

   e) What shape has been drawn? .... (1 mark)

   f) Comment on the diagonals of this shape.

   .... (1 mark)

3 Construct triangle LMN. LN = 6cm, $\angle L$ = 60° and $\angle N$ = 75°.

   a) Measure $\angle LMN$. .... (1 mark)

   b) Measure MN. .... (1 mark)

   c) Extend LN to P. Measure $\angle MNP$. .... (1 mark)

Score /11

1 The diagonal of a parallelogram, with sides 4.5cm and 7cm, measures 10cm.

Use a pair of compasses and a straight edge to draw this parallelogram accurately.

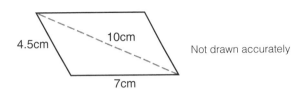

Not drawn accurately

(2 marks)

2 This is an isosceles trapezium with $AB = CD = 3.5$cm. $AD = 4$cm and $BC = 7$cm.

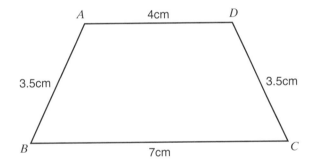

Open a pair of compasses to width over half of BC. Use points B and C to draw arcs crossing at E below BC.

a) What is the shape $ABECD$?

(1 mark)

b) Mark the midpoint (P) on AD. Join PE.

Mark the point (Q) where PE crosses BC.

Measure BQ and QC.

.... cm   (2 marks)

c) What do you notice about BQ, QC and the line PQE?

(1 mark)

Score   /6

For more help on this topic see KS3 Maths Revision Guide pages 60–61.

A **Choose just one answer, a, b, c or d.**

1 A triangle with three sides of different length and three different angles is: (1 mark)
a) equilateral
b) isosceles
c) right-angled
d) scalene

2 A quadrilateral with four sides of different length is a: (1 mark)
a) parallelogram
b) kite
c) trapezium
d) rhombus

3 A polygon with five sides of different length is a: (1 mark)
a) pentagon
b) regular pentagon
c) hexagon
d) regular hexagon

4 An angle inside a polygon is: (1 mark)
a) an interior angle
b) an exterior angle
c) a right angle
d) an obtuse angle

5 The sum of an interior angle and an exterior angle is: (1 mark)
a) 90°
b) 180°
c) 60°
d) 360°

Score /5

B **Answer all parts of each question.**

1 Name the following 2D shapes.
a) Eight equal sides .... (1 mark)
b) Two pairs of equal angles .... (1 mark)

2 a) What is the name of a triangle with two equal sides?
.... (1 mark)

b) i) Two of these triangles are joined by their shortest sides. What shape is made?
.... (1 mark)

ii) The diagonals measure 8cm and 4cm. Work out the area of the shape.
.... (1 mark)

3 a) A regular hexagon is divided into two halves. What is the shape of one half?
.... (1 mark)

b) i) On the original hexagon, number each vertex. A diagonal is drawn from vertex 1 to vertex 3. What shape is the smaller area?
.... (1 mark)

ii) What shape is the larger area?
.... (1 mark)

Score /8

Answer all parts of the questions. Use a separate sheet of paper if necessary.

1 Here are two shapes:

a) Are both shapes hexagons?

Tick (✓) Yes or No

☐ Yes   ☐ No

Explain your answer.

(1 mark)

b) Are both shapes regular?

Tick (✓) Yes or No

☐ Yes   ☐ No

Explain your answer.

(1 mark)

2 Complete this table about regular polygons.

Polygon	Side	Perimeter	Exterior angle	Interior angle
pentagon	6.5cm			
octagon	6.5cm	52cm		
decagon		50cm		

(2 marks)

3 Join dots to make a four-sided shape that has one pair of parallel sides. Name the shape.

(2 marks)

Score   /6

For more help on this topic see KS3 Maths Revision Guide pages 62–63.

| **A** | **Choose just one answer, a, b, c or d.** |

1 Name the transformation that moves a shape vertically and horizontally.

(1 mark)

a) reflection ☐
b) rotation ☐
c) translation ☐
d) enlargement ☐

2 Name the transformation that turns a shape about a point. (1 mark)

a) reflection ☐
b) rotation ☐
c) translation ☐
d) enlargement ☐

3 Name the transformation that produces a mirror image. (1 mark)

a) reflection ☐
b) rotation ☐
c) translation ☐
d) enlargement ☐

4 A mirror line is also called: (1 mark)

a) a line of symmetry ☐
b) a graph ☐
c) an axis ☐
d) a reflector ☐

5 A column vector describes: (1 mark)

a) movement at an angle ☐
b) single movement along a diagonal ☐
c) circular movement ☐
d) horizontal combined with vertical movement ☐

Score /5

| **B** | **Describe the transformations that move each of the following.** |

1 A → B

....

.... (1 mark)

2 B → C

....

.... (1 mark)

3 C → D

....

.... (1 mark)

4 D → A

....

.... (1 mark)

Score /4

Answer all parts of the questions. Use a separate sheet of paper if necessary.

1 When a rhombus is folded along a diagonal, a triangle is formed.

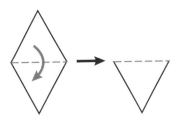

a) If a parallelogram is folded along a diagonal, what shape is made? Choose A, B or C.

A **B** **C**

(1 mark)

b) These shapes have been folded along the dotted line.

Draw and name each shape before the paper was folded.

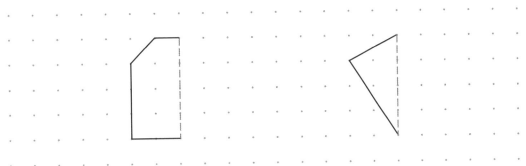

(2 marks)

2 The order of rotational symmetry is the number of times a shape turns in one revolution and still looks the same.

Circle the order of rotational symmetry for each of the following.

a) Child's windmill

3
4
5

b) Snowflake

6
5
4

c) Equilateral triangle

2
3
4

(3 marks)

Score   /6

For more help on this topic see KS3 Maths Revision Guide pages 64–65.

A Choose just one answer, a, b, c or d.

1 Triangles are congruent if: (1 mark)
   a) two sides and an angle are equal ☐
   b) two angles and a side are equal ☐
   c) one side and one angle are equal ☐
   d) two angles are equal ☐

2 Triangles are similar if: (1 mark)
   a) there is one right angle in each ☐
   b) one angle in each is equal ☐
   c) two sides are equal ☐
   d) three angles are equal ☐

3 If one triangle is an enlargement of another triangle: (1 mark)
   a) they are similar ☐
   b) they are congruent ☐
   c) they are the same size ☐
   d) they look the same size ☐

4 A scale factor greater than 1: (1 mark)
   a) keeps a shape the same ☐
   b) turns a shape around ☐
   c) enlarges a shape ☐
   d) reduces a shape ☐

5 A line through corresponding vertices of original and enlarged shapes goes through: (1 mark)
   a) the centre of enlargement ☐
   b) the origin ☐
   c) the centre of the original shape ☐
   d) the centre of the enlarged shape ☐

Score /5

B Answer all parts of each question.

1 a) Are triangle ABE and triangle ACD congruent or similar?

.... (1 mark)

b) What is the scale factor?

.... (1 mark)

c) Work out BE to 2 d.p.

.... cm (1 mark)

d) Work out DE to 2 d.p.

.... cm (1 mark)

2 A kite has two sides of 3cm and two sides of 5.6cm.

a) The kite is enlarged by a scale factor of 3.

What is the perimeter of the enlarged shape? .... cm (1 mark)

b) The kite is enlarged by a scale factor of $\frac{1}{2}$.

What is the perimeter of the enlarged shape? .... cm (1 mark)

Score /6

Answer all parts of the questions. Use a separate sheet of paper if necessary.

1 This diagram shows a cross-section through a roof.

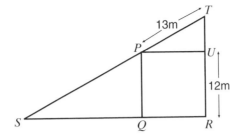

PQRU is a square with side measuring 12m.

The length of *TP* is 13m.

Show that the length of *PS* is 31.2m

Show all your working. 🖩

(3 marks)

2 Use the isometric grids provided for this question.

a) i) Draw a triangle.

ii) Draw a congruent triangle to make a larger triangle.

(1 mark)

iii) Add two more congruent triangles to make a parallelogram.

(1 mark)

b) i) Draw an isosceles trapezium.

ii) Draw a congruent trapezium to make a hexagon.

(1 mark)

Score /6

For more help on this topic see KS3 Maths Revision Guide pages 66–67.

A | Choose just one answer, a, b, c or d.

1 An angle between 90° and
180° is: (1 mark)
a) acute ☐ **b)** obtuse ☐
c) reflex ☐ **d)** interior ☐

2 An angle between N and
NE is: (1 mark)
a) acute ☐ **b)** obtuse ☐
c) reflex ☐ **d)** interior ☐

3 Angles on a straight line add
up to: (1 mark)
a) 360° ☐ **b)** 270° ☐
c) 90° ☐ **d)** 180° ☐

4 Three angles of 85° meet at a point.
The fourth angle is: (1 mark)
a) 105° ☐
b) 180° ☐
c) 215° ☐
d) 315° ☐

5 Allied angles add up to: (1 mark)
a) 360° ☐
b) 180° ☐
c) 100° ☐
d) 90° ☐

Score /5

B | Answer all parts of each question.

1 Two straight lines cross. Find the other three angles at their intersection if the
fourth angle is:

a) 32° .... (1 mark)

b) 110° .... (1 mark)

2 A pair of parallel lines is crossed by a straight line at X and Y. One angle is given.

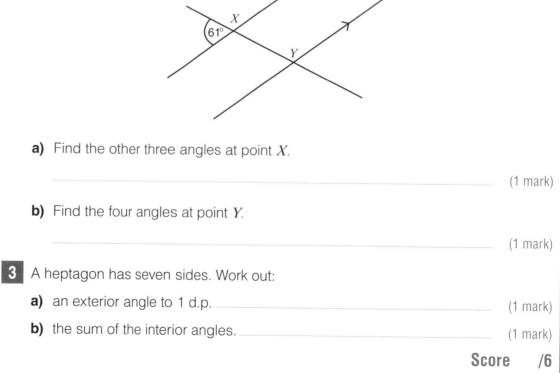

a) Find the other three angles at point X.

.... (1 mark)

b) Find the four angles at point Y.

.... (1 mark)

3 A heptagon has seven sides. Work out:

a) an exterior angle to 1 d.p. .... (1 mark)

b) the sum of the interior angles. .... (1 mark)

Score /6

Answer all parts of the questions. Use a separate sheet of paper if necessary.

1 Work out an exterior angle and the sum of the interior angles of these regular polygons.

 a) Octagon

Exterior angle = ... °

Sum of interior angles = ... ° (1 mark)

 b) Decagon

Exterior angle = ... °

Sum of interior angles = ... ° (1 mark)

2 A triangle has two acute angles and an obtuse angle:

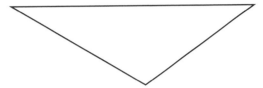

Not drawn accurately

The obtuse angle is three times the sum of the acute angles.

 a) Work out the obtuse angle.

.... ° (1 mark)

One acute angle is 15° more than the other acute angle.

 b) Work out both acute angles.

.... ° and .... ° (1 mark)

3 Two different quadrilaterals are fitted together to make a right-angled triangle.

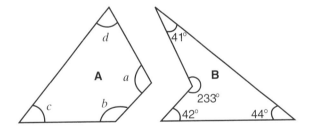

Not drawn accurately

The angles of quadrilateral **B** are given.

Work out the angles of quadrilateral **A**, giving reasons.

(2 marks)

Score **/6**

For more help on this topic see KS3 Maths Revision Guide pages 68–69.

A **Choose just one answer, a, b, c or d.**

1 Pythagoras' theorem can be used in: (1 mark)
- **a)** an acute-angled triangle ☐
- **b)** an obtuse-angled triangle ☐
- **c)** a right-angled triangle ☐
- **d)** an equilateral triangle ☐

2 The hypotenuse is the side opposite: (1 mark)
- **a)** the acute angle ☐
- **b)** the obtuse angle ☐
- **c)** any angle ☐
- **d)** the right angle ☐

3 Pythagoras' theorem is used to find: (1 mark)
- **a)** any angle ☐
- **b)** any side ☐
- **c)** the ratio of sides ☐
- **d)** the sum of angles ☐

4 The trigonometrical ratio not using the hypotenuse is: (1 mark)
- **a)** sine ☐
- **b)** tangent ☐
- **c)** cosine ☐
- **d)** inverse cosine ☐

5 Which of these triangles is right-angled? (1 mark)
- **a)** 3, 4, 6 ☐
- **b)** 6, 12, 13 ☐
- **c)** 7, 24, 25 ☐
- **d)** 9, 15, 17 ☐

Score /5

B **Answer all parts of these questions about right-angled triangles. The hypotenuse is the longest side.**

1 Find the missing length of the hypotenuse in these triangles. (2 marks)

a) 10mm, 24mm .... **b)** 15cm, 27cm ....

2 Find the missing length of the shortest side in these triangles. (2 marks)

a) 6cm, 6.5cm .... **b)** 9.5cm, 10cm ....

3 Are triangles with these sides right-angled? (2 marks)

a) 5.2cm, 3.6cm, 4.5cm .... **b)** 16mm, 30mm, 34mm ....

4 Find the missing side or angle in each of these triangles (to 1 d.p.).

a) $\angle P = 37°$, $PQ = 48$cm, $QR =$ .... (1 mark)

b) $PQ = 12.6$cm, $PR = 16.8$cm, $\angle R =$ .... (1 mark)

c) $\angle R = 73°$, $PR = 32$cm, $QR =$ .... (1 mark)

d) $PQ = 35.1$mm, $QR = 27.8$mm, $\angle P =$ .... (1 mark)

Score /10

Answer all parts of the questions. Use a separate sheet of paper if necessary.

1 Is it possible to have a triangle with this angle and these lengths?

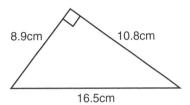

Show all your working. 🖩

(2 marks)

2 Work out the length of side AB in this triangle, giving your answer to 1 decimal place. 🖩

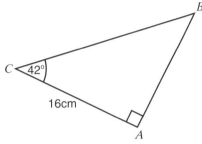

Not drawn accurately

$AB =$ _____ cm   (1 mark)

3 PQR is a right-angled triangle. 🖩

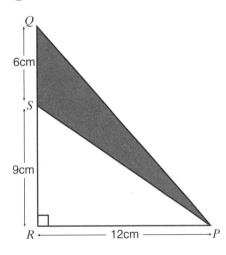

Not drawn accurately

a) What is the area of the shaded triangle PQS?

_____ cm² (1 mark)

b) Work out the length PS.

_____ cm (1 mark)

c) Find $\angle PQR$.

_____ ° (1 mark)

Score   /6

For more help on this topic see KS3 Maths Revision Guide pages 70–71.

A Choose just one answer, a, b, c or d.

1 How many vertices does a cuboid have? (1 mark)
a) 4 ☐ b) 6 ☐
c) 10 ☐ d) 8 ☐

2 How many edges does a triangular prism have? (1 mark)
a) 9 ☐ b) 8 ☐
c) 6 ☐ d) 10 ☐

3 How many faces does a tetrahedron have? (1 mark)
a) 3 ☐ b) 5 ☐
c) 4 ☐ d) 6 ☐

4 The volume of a cone is found by: (1 mark)
a) $V = \pi r^2 h$ ☐
b) $V = \frac{1}{3}\pi r^2 h$ ☐
c) $V = \frac{4}{3}\pi r^2 h$ ☐
d) $V = lbw$ ☐

5 A cone is a pyramid with a base that is in the shape of a: (1 mark)
a) triangle ☐ b) square ☐
c) circle ☐ d) rectangle ☐

Score   /5

B Answer all parts of each question. Use the π key on your calculator.

1 A hollow sphere, diameter 5cm, is to be painted.

a) What is the area to be painted to 1 d.p.? .... cm² (1 mark)

b) A half-litre tin of paint can cover 5m². How many spheres can be painted from one tin of paint?

.... (1 mark)

c) What is the air capacity of the sphere? .... cm³ (1 mark)

2 A solid shape is made from a cylinder (height 7cm) with a cone (diameter 1.6cm, height 2.5cm) on each end.

Work out the following, remembering to use the slant height.

a) Volume of the whole shape (to 2 d.p.) .... cm³ (1 mark)

b) Surface area of the whole shape (to 2 d.p.) .... cm² (1 mark)

3 A cake is made of three round layers.

The diameters and heights are in the ratio 5 : 3 : 2

The cake's bottom layer has a diameter of 30cm and a height of 10cm.

Work out the following, giving your answers to the nearest whole number.

a) The height of the whole cake .... cm (1 mark)

b) The volume of the whole cake .... cm³ (1 mark)

c) The area of icing needed for the whole cake .... cm² (1 mark)

Score   /8

Answer all parts of the questions. Use a separate sheet of paper if necessary.

1 A child has made this cuboid out of identical plastic cubes:

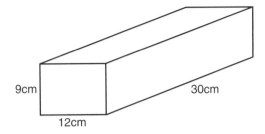

9cm   30cm   12cm

The cubes have edges of 30mm.

How many cubes were used to build the cuboid?

Show all your working.

(2 marks)

2 This carton holds a solid block of chocolate:

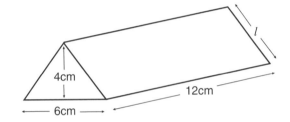

4cm   6cm   12cm   *l*

a) What is the volume of chocolate in the carton?

Show all your working.

.... cm³   (2 marks)

b) The chocolate is completely covered by tin foil.

What is the area of tin foil covering the chocolate?

Show all your working.

.... cm²   (2 marks)

3 A vase, 20cm high, is made from two cylinders, one inside the other. The outer cylinder has a diameter of 10cm. There is a space of 2cm between the sides and bases of the cylinders.

Work out the capacity of the inner cylinder, giving your answer to 1 decimal place. ▦

.... cm³   (2 marks)

Score   /8

For more help on this topic see KS3 Maths Revision Guide pages 72–73.

A Choose just one answer, a, b, c or d.

1 The sum of the probabilities of all possible outcomes equals: (1 mark)
a) 0.5 ☐ b) 1 ☐
c) 1.5 ☐ d) 2 ☐

2 The probability of an 'evens' event equals: (1 mark)
a) 0.5 ☐ b) 0.25 ☐
c) 0.15 ☐ d) 0.6 ☐

3 An unlikely event has a probability (P) with: (1 mark)
a) $0.5 < P < 1$ ☐
b) $0.2 < P < 0.4$ ☐
c) $0.1 < P < 0.5$ ☐
d) $0 < P < 0.5$ ☐

4 The probability of getting two heads when tossing two coins is: (1 mark)
a) $\frac{1}{2}$ ☐ b) $\frac{1}{3}$ ☐
c) $\frac{1}{4}$ ☐ d) $\frac{3}{4}$ ☐

5 The probability of **not** getting two heads when tossing two coins is: (1 mark)
a) $\frac{1}{4}$ ☐ b) $\frac{1}{2}$ ☐
c) $\frac{3}{4}$ ☐ d) $\frac{1}{3}$ ☐

Score /5

B Answer all parts of each question.

1 Two dice are thrown together and their scores added. Work out the probability of these scores.
a) P(odd number) .... (1 mark)
b) P($\geq$ 10) .... (1 mark)
c) P(multiple of 3) .... (1 mark)

2 The letters of the word **IMPOSSIBLE** are each written on cards.
A card is picked at random. Work out the following probabilities.
a) P(**I**) .... (1 mark)
b) P(vowel) .... (1 mark)
c) P(**X**, **Y**, **Z**) .... (1 mark)

3 A tin of assorted biscuits contains 4 plain biscuits, 5 chocolate biscuits, 3 cream biscuits and 6 shortbread.
A biscuit is chosen. Work out the following probabilities.
a) P(shortbread) .... (1 mark)
b) P(not chocolate) .... (1 mark)

4 A spinner has 8 possible outcomes: 4 red, 3 blue, 1 white. It is spun once. Work out:
a) P(blue) .... (1 mark)
b) P(not white) .... (1 mark)

Score /10

Answer all parts of the questions. Use a separate sheet of paper if necessary.

1 A Portuguese word game uses 120 tiles. The four letters with the most number of tiles are:

A	E	I	O
14	11	10	10

One tile is picked at random.

a) What is the probability it will be A, E, I or O?

(2 marks)

b) What is the probability that I or O will not be picked?

(2 marks)

c) The probability of picking P, R or S is $\frac{3}{20}$.

The ratio of tiles P : R : S = 2 : 3 : 4

How many P, R and S tiles are each in the game?

P tiles = ...

R tiles = ...

S tiles = ... (3 marks)

2 If the probability of a girl winning a game is $\frac{5}{12}$, is she more likely to win or lose the game?

Tick (✓) Win or Lose.

☐ Win   ☐ Lose

Explain your answer.

(1 mark)

3 There are five counters in a bag. They each have a different positive integer marked on them.

A counter is picked at random.

P(odd number) = 0

P(number ≤ 10) = 1

What are the numbers on the counters?

(2 marks)

Score   /10

For more help on this topic see KS3 Maths Revision Guide pages 76–77.

A

A card is picked at random from a pack of playing cards. Find these probabilities. Choose just one answer, a, b, c or d.

1 P(King) = (1 mark)

a) $\frac{1}{4}$ ☐   b) $\frac{1}{13}$ ☐

c) $\frac{4}{13}$ ☐   d) $\frac{1}{2}$ ☐

2 P(picture card) = (1 mark)

a) $\frac{3}{13}$ ☐   b) $\frac{1}{4}$ ☐

c) $\frac{4}{13}$ ☐   d) $\frac{6}{13}$ ☐

3 P(red card) = (1 mark)

a) $\frac{1}{2}$ ☐   b) $\frac{1}{4}$ ☐

c) $\frac{3}{4}$ ☐   d) $\frac{1}{3}$ ☐

4 P(not an ace) = (1 mark)

a) $\frac{9}{13}$ ☐   b) $\frac{10}{13}$ ☐

c) $\frac{12}{13}$ ☐   d) $\frac{7}{8}$ ☐

5 P(an even-number card) = (1 mark)

a) $\frac{5}{13}$ ☐   b) $\frac{11}{13}$ ☐

c) $\frac{12}{13}$ ☐   d) $\frac{3}{4}$ ☐

Score /5

B

Answer each question. Use a separate sheet of paper as necessary.

1 A box of chocolates contains 10 soft centres, 12 hard centres and 3 plain chocolates.

Work out the following probabilities. In part **b)**, assume the two chocolates are taken out of the box together (i.e. **not** one after the other).

a) P(hard centre) (1 mark)

b) P(hard centre and soft centre) (1 mark)

c) P(soft centre or plain chocolate) (1 mark)

2 A fair spinner has four outcomes: red, blue, green, yellow. It is spun once and a fair dice is thrown at the same time.

Using a sample space diagram to display all possible outcomes, work out:

a) P(even/green) (1 mark)

b) P(odd/not yellow) (1 mark)

3 A bag has five 50p coins and four £1 coins.

A coin is picked at random and not replaced. A second coin is picked at random.

Using a probability tree to display all possible outcomes, work out:

a) P(two coins the same) (1 mark)

b) P(no £1 coins) (1 mark)

Score /7

1   These are two four-sided shapes. They are numbered 2, 4, 6, 8 and 1, 2, 3, 4.

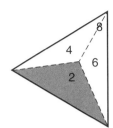 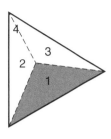

The shapes are both thrown and their scores are added.

Use a sample space diagram to show all possible outcomes.

What is the probability that the total is even?

(2 marks)

2   A bowl of fruit is handed round. In the bowl are four red plums and three yellow plums.

   a)   Use a probability tree to work out all the different ways two plums can be picked. They are eaten, so cannot be replaced.

(2 marks)

   b)   What is the probability of choosing two plums of the same colour?

(1 mark)

   c)   What is the probability of not choosing a yellow plum?

(1 mark)

3   The probability that a girl is late for school on a Thursday is 0.2

The probability that she is late for school on a Friday is 0.3

Work out the probability that she is late for school on only one of these days.

(2 marks)

Score   /8

For more help on this topic see KS3 Maths Revision Guide pages 78–79.

A Choose just one answer, a, b, c or d.

1 How many members are in the set of primes < 20? (1 mark)
a) 5 ☐   b) 6 ☐
c) 7 ☐   d) 8 ☐

2 How many even members are in the set of primes < 20? (1 mark)
a) 1 ☐   b) 2 ☐
c) 3 ☐   d) 4 ☐

3 How many multiples of 6 are in the set of integers < 100? (1 mark)
a) 13 ☐   b) 14 ☐
c) 15 ☐   d) 16 ☐

4 An infinite set has how many members? (1 mark)
a) unlimited ☐
b) 1000 ☐
c) 1 000 000 ☐
d) none ☐

5 The intersection of sets is shown by which symbol? (1 mark)
a) ∪ ☐
b) ∩ ☐
c) ∅ ☐
d) ε ☐

Score   /5

B Answer all parts of each question.

1 This Venn diagram gives information about families living in a block of flats and using online supermarket deliveries.

a) How many flats use supermarket R delivery?
.... (1 mark)

b) How many flats have deliveries from both supermarkets S and T?
.... (1 mark)

c) How many flats have deliveries from all three supermarkets?
.... (1 mark)

d) How many flats are in the block?
.... (1 mark)

2 S is the set of squared numbers < 150. C is the set of cubed numbers < 150.

a) List the members of S∪C. .... (1 mark)

b) List the members of S∩C. .... (1 mark)

c) List the members of S∪C subset of even numbers. .... (1 mark)

3 P is the set of factors of 28. Q is the set of factors of 40.

a) List the members of P∩Q. .... (1 mark)

b) What is the HCF of 28 and 40? .... (1 mark)

Score   /9

Answer all parts of the questions. Use a separate sheet of paper if necessary.

1 Set N = {all numbers from 1 to 100}

List the members of the following subsets of Set N.

a) F = {factors of 64}

(1 mark)

b) M = {multiples of 9}

(1 mark)

c) P = {primes ending in 9}

(1 mark)

2 A group of students are asked how they read books.

This Venn diagram illustrates the results.

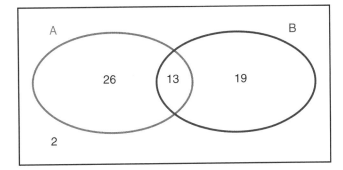

Set A use an e-reader. Set B read 'hardcopy' books.

a) How many students use an e-reader?

(1 mark)

b) How many students use both methods?

(1 mark)

c) How many students were questioned?

(1 mark)

d) Suggest a reason why two students are not in Set A or Set B.

(1 mark)

Score /7

For more help on this topic see KS3 Maths Revision Guide pages 80–81.

A Choose just one answer, a, b, c or d.

1 What sort of data gives shoe sizes? (1 mark)
a) theoretical ☐ **b)** grouped ☐
c) discrete ☐ **d)** continuous ☐

2 What sort of data gives the height of sunflowers? (1 mark)
a) theoretical ☐ **b)** grouped ☐
c) discrete ☐ **d)** continuous ☐

3 Which of these is continuous data? (1 mark)
a) types of coffee sold in a shop ☐
b) favourite flowers in a florist ☐
c) weights of fish caught in a river ☐
d) age groups of gym members ☐

4 Which of the following is grouped discrete data? (1 mark)
a) weights of babies in a clinic ☐
b) numbers of grapes on bunches on a vine ☐
c) heights of tulips in a garden ☐
d) travel times ☐

5 Which of the following is discrete data? (1 mark)
a) length of shelves in a library ☐
b) weights of books in a library ☐
c) size of books in a library ☐
d) types of books in a library ☐

Score /5

B Answer all parts of each question.

1 These are three questions from a questionnaire about the popularity of TV programmes. Rewrite the questions to make them more suitable.

a) Are you young or old?

.... (1 mark)

b) Do you watch TV in the evening?

.... (1 mark)

c) Is 'The Main Chance' any good?

.... (1 mark)

2 This tally chart shows the favourite English cheeses of some supermarket customers:

Cheese	Red Leicester	Cheddar	Cheshire	Lancashire	Wensleydale
Frequency	ЖI ЖI ЖI II	ЖI ЖI ЖI ЖI ЖI ЖI ЖI	ЖI ЖI ЖI ЖI ЖI ЖI	ЖI ЖI ЖI ЖI ЖI III	ЖI ЖI ЖI

a) Complete this frequency table. (2 marks)

Cheese					
Frequency					

b) How many customers were questioned? .... (1 mark)

c) Which was the most popular English cheese? .... (1 mark)

Score /7

Answer all parts of the questions. Use a separate sheet of paper if necessary.

1 This table shows information about students in a school year.

	Right-handed	Left-handed
Boys	38	8
Girls	44	6

Use the table to write down what these numbers represent. The first is done for you.

There are 6 left-handed girls.

There are 38 ....

There are 14 ....

There are 96 ....

(2 marks)

2 A survey is being held to find out where people shop.

The number of customers going into the local newsagent's shop is recorded.

a) Give three reasons why this might not be a good place to record shoppers.

1. ....

2. ....

3. ....

(1 mark)

b) Suggest a place that might be more useful for answering the survey.

(1 mark)

c) Suggest who might find the results of the survey useful.

(1 mark)

Score /5

For more help on this topic see KS3 Maths Revision Guide pages 84–85.

A Choose just one answer, a, b, c or d.

1 Which average uses the middle value? (1 mark)
- **a)** mean ☐
- **b)** mode ☐
- **c)** median ☐
- **d)** range ☐

2 Which average uses the most frequent value? (1 mark)
- **a)** mean ☐
- **b)** mode ☐
- **c)** median ☐
- **d)** range ☐

3 Which average uses all values? (1 mark)
- **a)** mean ☐
- **b)** mode ☐
- **c)** median ☐
- **d)** range ☐

4 Which measure uses the difference between extreme values? (1 mark)
- **a)** mean ☐
- **b)** mode ☐
- **c)** median ☐
- **d)** range ☐

5 In a leap year, the mean number of days in a month is: (1 mark)
- **a)** 30 ☐
- **b)** 30.5 ☐
- **c)** 31 ☐
- **d)** 31.5 ☐

Score   /5

B Answer all parts of each question.

1 Everyone in a school year is asked if they have any pets and how many pets they have. This was the frequency table produced:

Number of pets	0	1	2	3	4
Frequency	28	25	31	24	12

- **a)** How many students were questioned? .... (1 mark)
- **b)** What was the modal number of pets? .... (1 mark)
- **c)** Work out the mean number of pets. .... (1 mark)
- **d)** What was the median number of pets? .... (1 mark)

2 These are the marks in a Physics test:

59	54	38	66	72	70	63	81	74	66	66	72

Work out the:

- **a)** mean mark .... (1 mark)
- **b)** modal mark .... (1 mark)
- **c)** median mark .... (1 mark)
- **d)** Which is the most appropriate average? Give reasons.

....

.... (2 marks)

Score   /9

Answer all parts of the questions. Use a separate sheet of paper if necessary.

1 A box holds 12 bags of raisins. The mean number of raisins in each bag is 42.

This table gives the number of raisins in 11 of the bags.

Number	Frequency
39	2
40	0
41	3
42	2
43	3
44	1

How many raisins are in the twelfth bag?

Show all your working. 🔢

(2 marks)

2 **a)** Four people in a family have these shoe sizes:

3   4   6   9

What is the median shoe size in the family?

(1 mark)

b) This table shows the shoe sizes of a group of students. 🔢

Size	Number of students
2	1
3	2
4	10
5	21
6	16
7	2

i) What are the median and modal shoe sizes of the group?

(1 mark)

ii) Work out the mean shoe size of the group.

(2 marks)

iii) Tick (✓) the best average to use for the group, giving a reason.

☐ Mean   ☐ Median   ☐ Mode

(1 mark)

Score   /7

For more help on this topic see KS3 Maths Revision Guide pages 86–87.

A — Choose just one answer, a, b, c or d.

1 What is the sum of the angles in a pie chart? *(1 mark)*
a) 900° ☐ b) 180° ☐
c) 360° ☐ d) 100° ☐

2 Pictures illustrate data in a: *(1 mark)*
a) bar chart ☐
b) scatter graph ☐
c) stem and leaf diagram ☐
d) pictogram ☐

3 In a bar chart, the bar length represents: *(1 mark)*
a) type ☐ b) width ☐
c) frequency ☐ d) item ☐

4 An angle of 72° in a pie chart represents what percentage of data? *(1 mark)*
a) 10% ☐
b) 20% ☐
c) 30% ☐
d) 40% ☐

5 If two sets of data increase together, their correlation is: *(1 mark)*
a) zero ☐
b) positive ☐
c) negative ☐
d) variable ☐

Score /5

B — Answer all parts of each question.

1 Draw a pie chart on a separate sheet of paper to illustrate this data. *(3 marks)*

Favourite sport	Football	Tennis	Swimming	Netball
Frequency	32	24	28	16

2 Look at this scatter graph, which shows test marks in Geography and History.

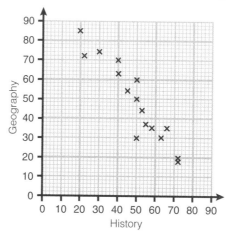

a) What correlation is shown? .... *(1 mark)*

b) Use a line of best fit to estimate the Geography mark for a student who scored 68 in History.

.... *(1 mark)*

Score /5

Answer all parts of the questions. Use a separate sheet of paper if necessary.

1 This chart shows the number of €10, €20 and €50 notes that were printed in 2011, 2012 and 2013.

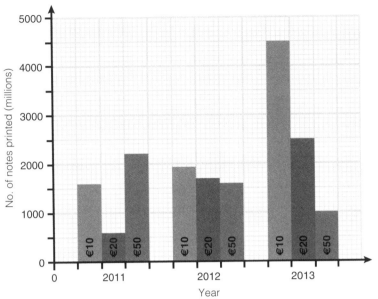

a) How many €20 notes were printed in 2012?

(1 mark)

b) In which year were the most €50 notes printed?

(1 mark)

c) What was the total number of €10 notes printed in the three years?

(1 mark)

2 This stem and leaf diagram shows the heights of 30 gladioli plants.

6	0 0
7	0 0 5 6
8	6 7 7 9
9	0 0 0 6 8
10	0 0 3 6 8 8 9
11	5 5 6 6
12	0 0 4 5

Key: 7 | 6 represents 76cm

a) What is the median height of the plants?

.... cm   (1 mark)

b) A gardening book says that the average gladioli grows to a height of 90cm.

What percentage of these plants did not reach the average height?

(2 marks)

Score   /6

For more help on this topic see KS3 Maths Revision Guide pages 88–89.

These questions should be answered without a calculator. The pencil icon indicates where to show your working and write your answer.

1 The star sign Gemini covers the dates May 21 to June 21 inclusive.

a) How many days is this?

.... days **(1 mark)**

b) A leap year has 366 days.

What fraction of a leap year is the Gemini period?

(1 mark)

2 A family has invited friends to a barbecue. There will be a total of 15 people.

The family has a menu for six people giving the following quantities.

Burgers: 6	Baked potatoes: 6
Steaks: 1kg	Coleslaw: 750g
Sausages: 700g	Baked beans: 160g
Barbecue sauce: 300ml	

What quantities would be needed for 15 people?

Burgers: ....   Baked potatoes: ....

Steaks: .... kg   Coleslaw: .... g

Sausages: .... g   Baked beans: .... g

Barbecue sauce: .... ml

(3 marks)

3 A straight line has the equation $9x + 3y = 15$

a) Write the equation in the form $y = mx + c$

(1 mark)

b) Use part **a)** to find the gradient and the coordinates of the point where the line crosses the y-axis.

(1 mark)

c) There is another parallel line passing through the point (2, 3).

Write down its equation.

(2 marks)

4 Two people, L and M, travel from A to B along different routes, but their journeys take the same time.

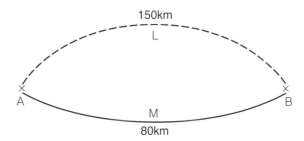

L travels at an average speed of 60km/h.

What is M's average speed?

.... km/h   **(3 marks)**

5 The perimeter of a triangle is 50cm.

The longest side is y cm.

The shortest side is 13cm shorter than the longest side.

The third side is 7cm longer than the shortest side.

a) Write an expression in y for each side.

(2 marks)

b) Form an equation in y and solve to find all three sides of the triangle.

(3 marks)

6 Four cuboids are made from 20 cubes.

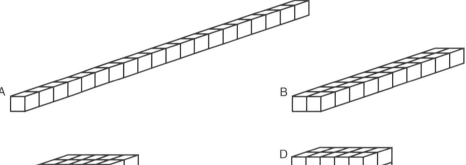

a) Write the missing information in this table of dimensions.

Cuboid	Dimensions		
A	20	1	1
B			
C			
D			

(2 marks)

b) Which cuboid has the largest surface area? Explain your answer.

Cuboid: .... **(2 marks)**

c) Work out the volume of each cuboid. Comment on the results.

(2 marks)

7 The heights of a group of five-year-olds were measured when they started school.

The results are shown in this stem and leaf diagram.

```
10 | 0   0   3   6   8   8   8   9
11 | 0   0   0   0   1   1   2   2   2   3   5   5   7   8   8   9
12 | 0   1   1   2
```

Key: 11 | 2 represents 112cm

a) How many children were in the group?

.... children   **(1 mark)**

b) What was the modal height?

.... cm   **(1 mark)**

c) What was the median height?

.... cm   **(2 marks)**

d) What was the range of heights?

.... cm   **(1 mark)**

8 A greengrocer takes delivery of a box of 40 pears and a box of 60 plums.

When he unpacks the fruit, he finds that 2 pears are rotten and 4 plums are mouldy.

a) What is the probability of picking out a good plum from the box?

(1 mark)

b) What is the probability of picking out a good pear and a mouldy plum from the boxes?

(2 marks)

c) The greengrocer arranges all the good fruit in a display.

What is the ratio of pears to plums in the display?

(1 mark)

9 A rectangle has an area of $15a^2$ cm^2 and a perimeter of $16a$ cm.

What are the dimensions of this rectangle?

Length = ... cm   Width = ... cm   **(2 marks)**

10 This scatter graph shows the average length of body and feet of a species of small animal.

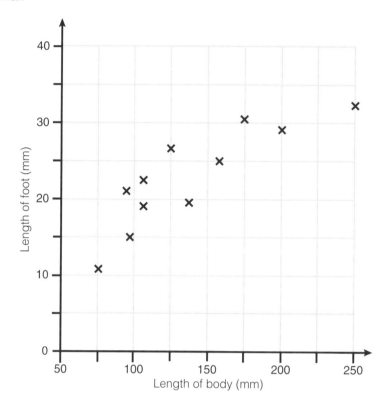

a) What relationship is there between the two measurements?

(1 mark)

b) Use a line of best fit to estimate the foot length if the body is 225mm long.

.... mm

(1 mark)

c) Another animal has these measurements: body 230mm, feet 18mm

Is it likely to be the same species?

Tick (✔) Yes or No   ☐ Yes   ☐ No

Explain your answer.

(1 mark)

11 A and B are two sets.

$$A = \{\text{multiples of 5}\} \qquad B = \{\text{multiples of 3}\}$$

List the four smallest members of:

a) $A \cup B$

(1 mark)

b) $A \cap B$

(1 mark)

12 These numbers and letters may have line symmetry, rotational symmetry or no symmetry.

Circle any type of symmetry possessed by each of these numbers and letters.

8	line symmetry	rotational symmetry	no symmetry
P	line symmetry	rotational symmetry	no symmetry
Z	line symmetry	rotational symmetry	no symmetry
6	line symmetry	rotational symmetry	no symmetry
Y	line symmetry	rotational symmetry	no symmetry

(2 marks)

A calculator can be used to answer these questions. ▣

13 A box-office hit film sold 50 121 601 tickets in the year it was released.

a) Round the number of tickets to 1 significant figure and then write it in standard form.

(2 marks)

These ticket sales gave the film a gross income of $408 992 272.

b) Write the gross income correct to 3 significant figures.

$ .... **(1 mark)**

The contract of the main star of the film gives him 15% of gross takings.

c) How much would he earn from the film's gross income to the nearest $100?

$ .... **(2 marks)**

14 Use your calculator to find the value of:

$$\frac{8.92^2 \times \sqrt{4.5}}{65.8 - 8.3}$$

a) Write down the whole calculator display.

(1 mark)

b) Without using a calculator, show how to check the answer is of the correct magnitude.

(1 mark)

15 The formula $C = \frac{5}{9}(F - 32)$ converts temperatures from the Fahrenheit scale to Celsius.

a) On a certain day the temperature in Moscow is 35.6°F

Work out the temperature in the Celsius scale.

.... °C **(1 mark)**

b) On the same day the temperature in Tenerife is 23°C

Work out the temperature in the Fahrenheit scale.

.... °F **(1 mark)**

The minute hand on a clock face measures 12.5cm from the centre of the clock face to the tip.

Work out the distance, correct to 1 decimal place, that the tip travels in:

a) 20 minutes

.... cm   **(1 mark)**

b) 45 minutes

.... cm   **(1 mark)**

c) one day

.... cm   **(2 marks)**

17 This shape is made from two similar triangles.

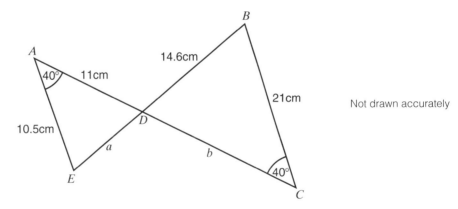

Not drawn accurately

a) Work out the missing sides a and b.

$a =$ .... cm $b =$ .... cm   **(2 marks)**

b) $\angle A$ and $\angle C$ both equal 40°. What does this tell you about lines AE and BC?

(1 mark)

18 A pet shop sells a tropical fish tank for £99. Its dimensions are length = 53cm, height = 41cm, width = 31cm.

a) What is the capacity of the fish tank?

.... cm³ **(1 mark)**

b) The water is filled up to 4cm from the top. How much water is in the tank?

.... cm³ **(1 mark)**

c) The tank holds four fish of one variety, costing £1.55 each, and two fish of another variety, costing £2.10 each. There is also a small snail, costing £2.49, in the tank.

The customer gave the cashier £120. How much change did the customer receive?

Change: £ .... **(2 marks)**

19 A new sample book of designs is being produced, using different scales.

Complete this table giving design dimensions and actual measurements for different scales.

Scale	Design dimension	Actual dimension
1 : 10	6.4cm	
1 : 8		1.36m
	20cm	4m
	9cm	22.5cm
1 : 250	4.8cm	
1 : 75		825cm

(3 marks)

20 Some PE students are testing the bounce of tennis balls. They record the height of the bounce of six tennis balls as follows:

625mm   60.1cm   64cm   0.6m   613mm   0.642m

a) What is the range of the bounce heights in millimetres?

.... mm **(1 mark)**

b) What was the mean height recorded in millimetres to 2 decimal places?

.... mm **(2 marks)**